Hermes Alegre
Art Gallery Book - 2
September, 2014

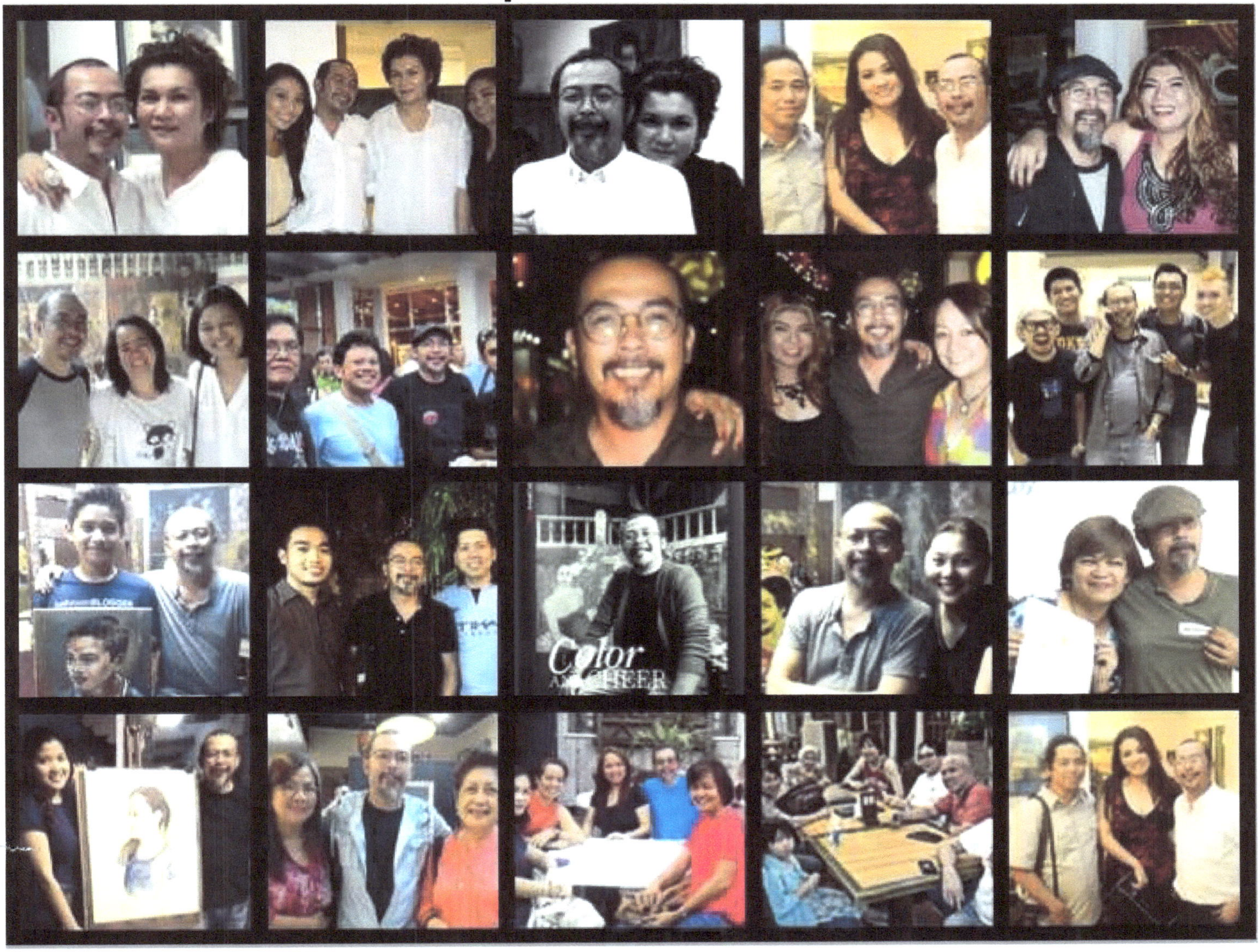

Welcome to Hermes Alegre Art Gallery Book-2, size 8.5x11 inches. Hermes hails from Daet, Camarines Norte and has created great excitement in the art world with his wonderful paintings for more than 20 years.

He finished his Arts degree from PWU in Manila. His latest art show was done in NY City in mid 2011, together with his fellow artists. The purpose of this art book is to maximize exposure of his art work. Please contact his face book account under his name in case you are interested to order his works or commission him to paint for you. Copies of this book are available online and via self-publisher.

Due to his many paintings, hopefully further sequels of this book will be made. You can frame any of the paintings and hang them in walls, by buying extra copies of this book, which is very affordable.

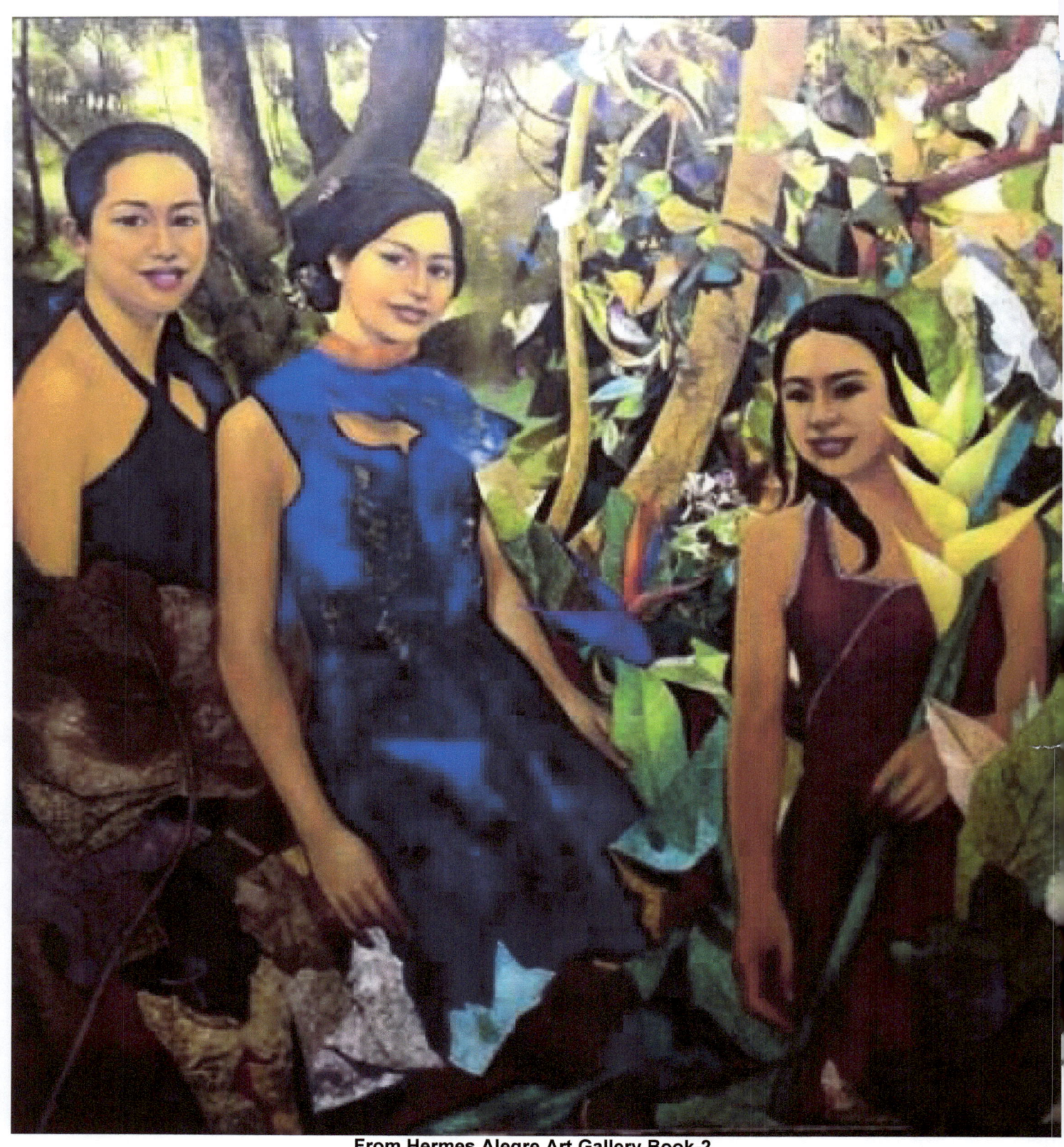

From Hermes Alegre Art Gallery Book-2

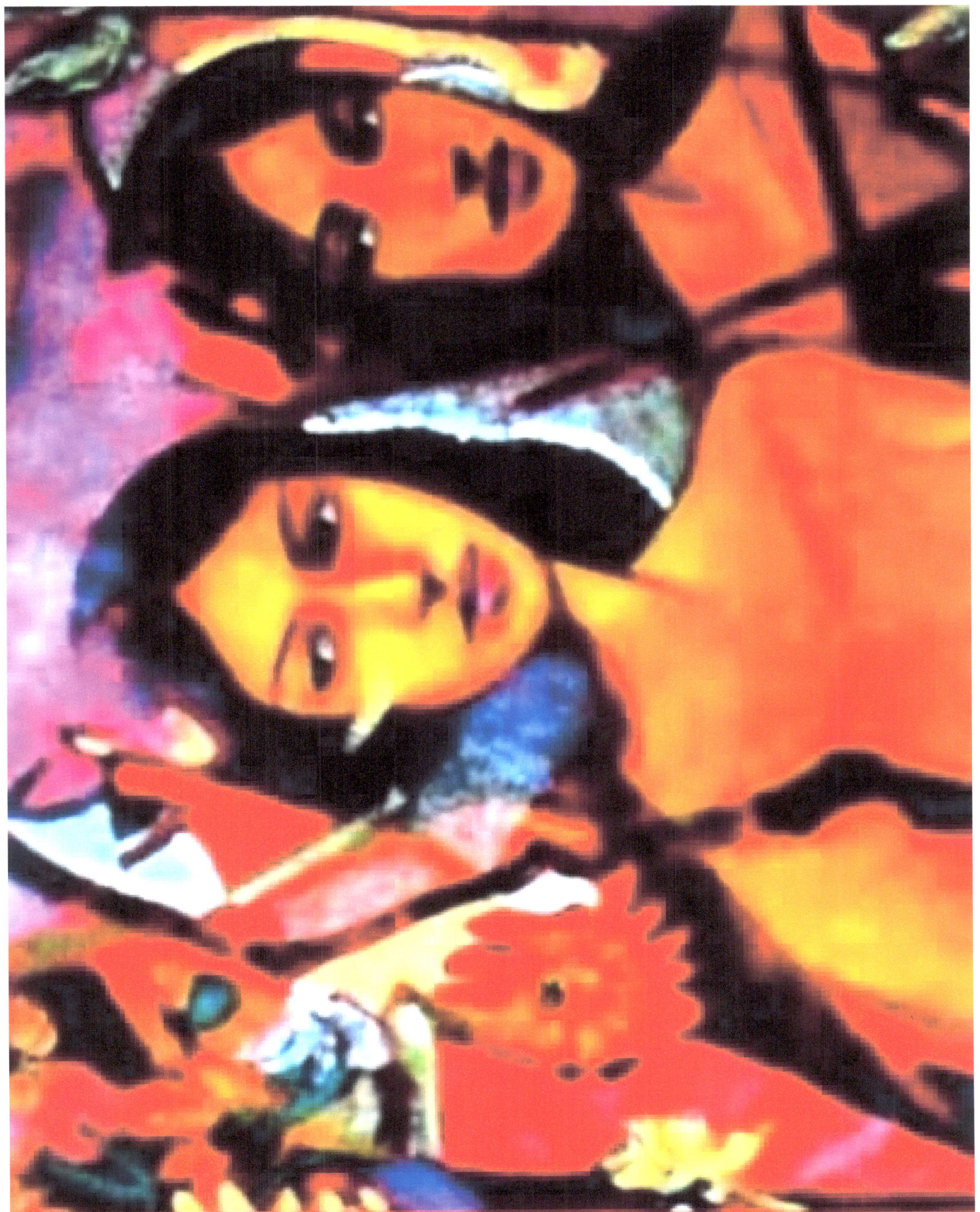

From Hermes Alegre Art Gallery Book-2

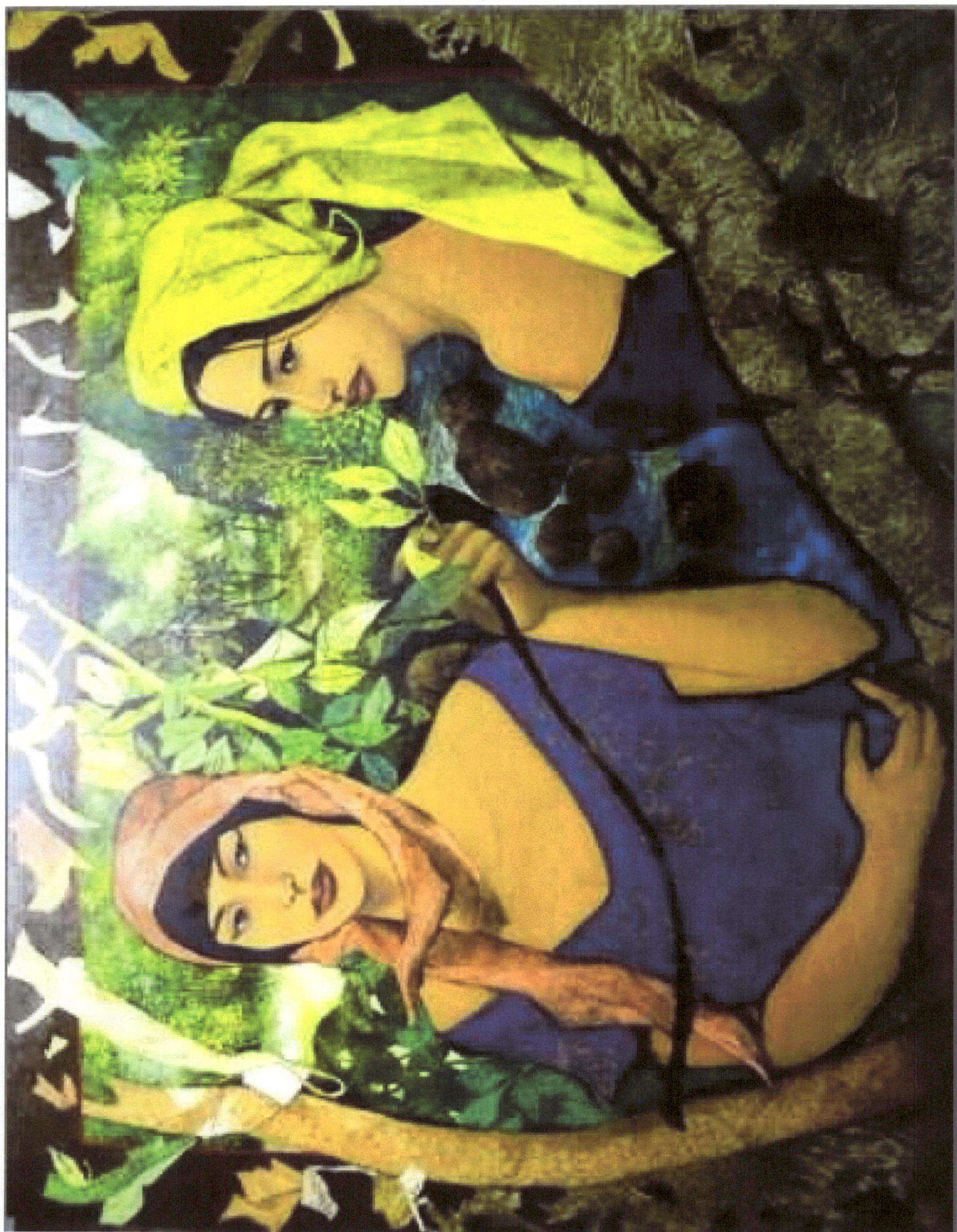

From Hermes Alegre Art Gallery Book-2

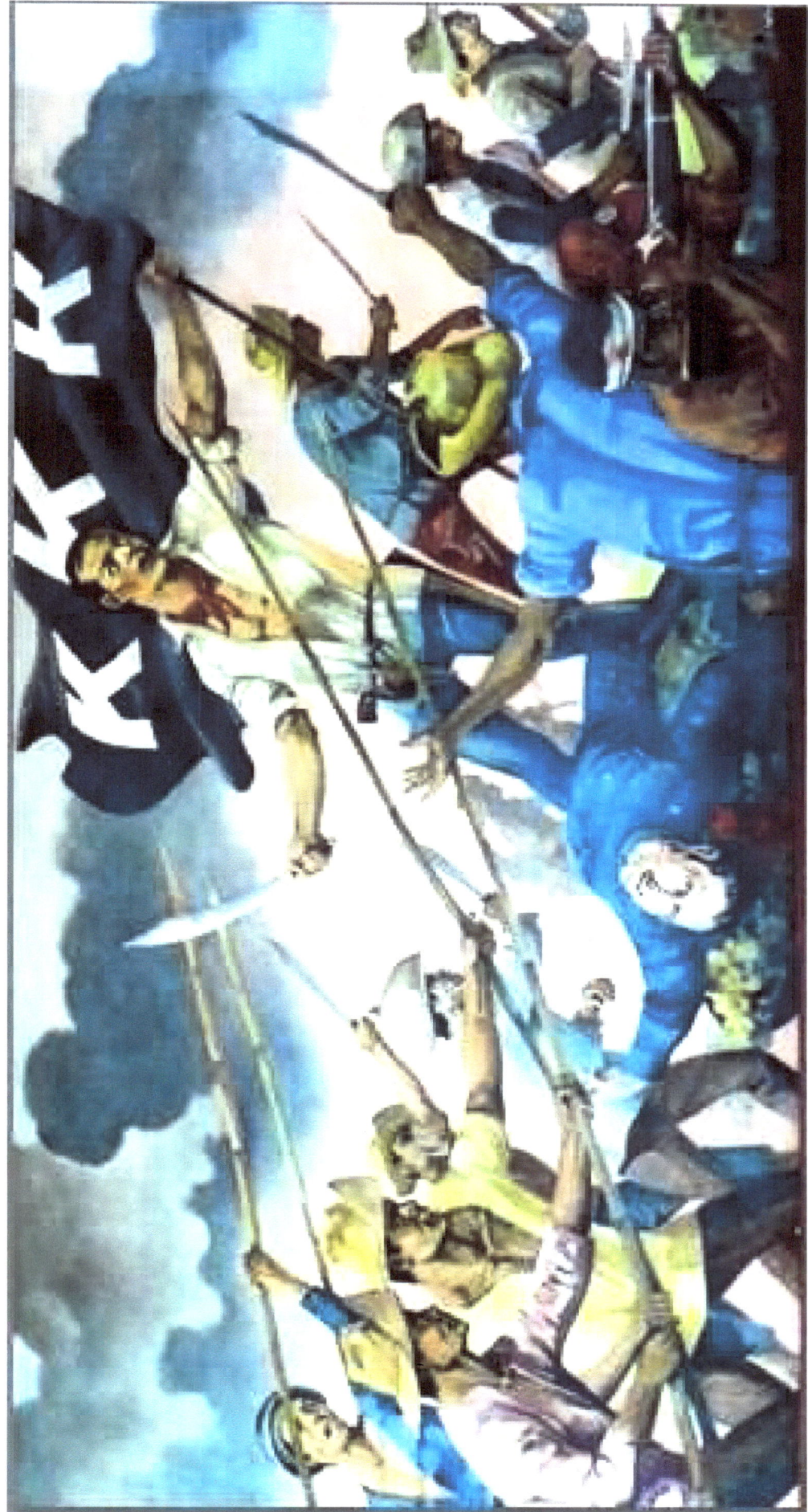

From Hermes Alegre Art Gallery Book-2

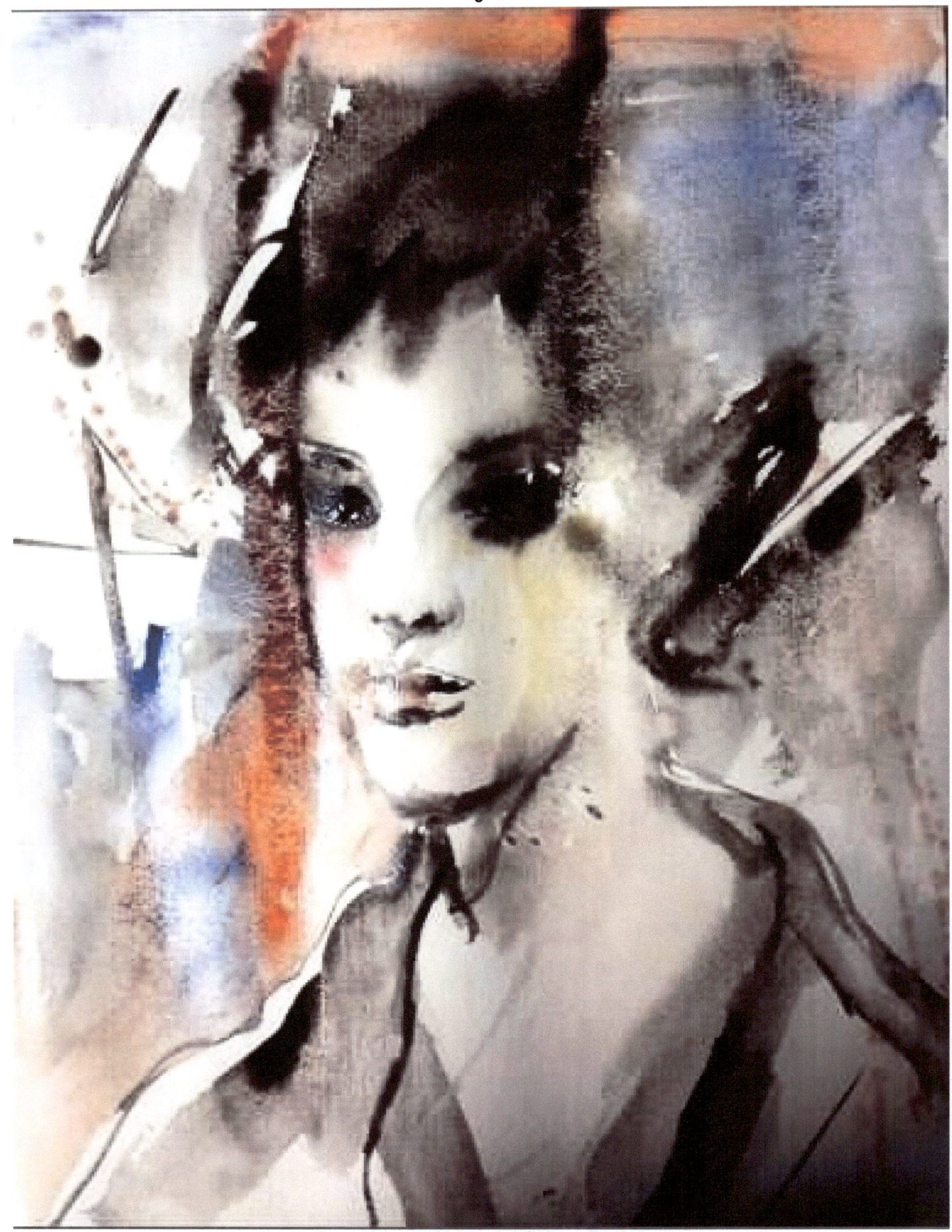

From Hermes Alegre Art Gallery Book-2

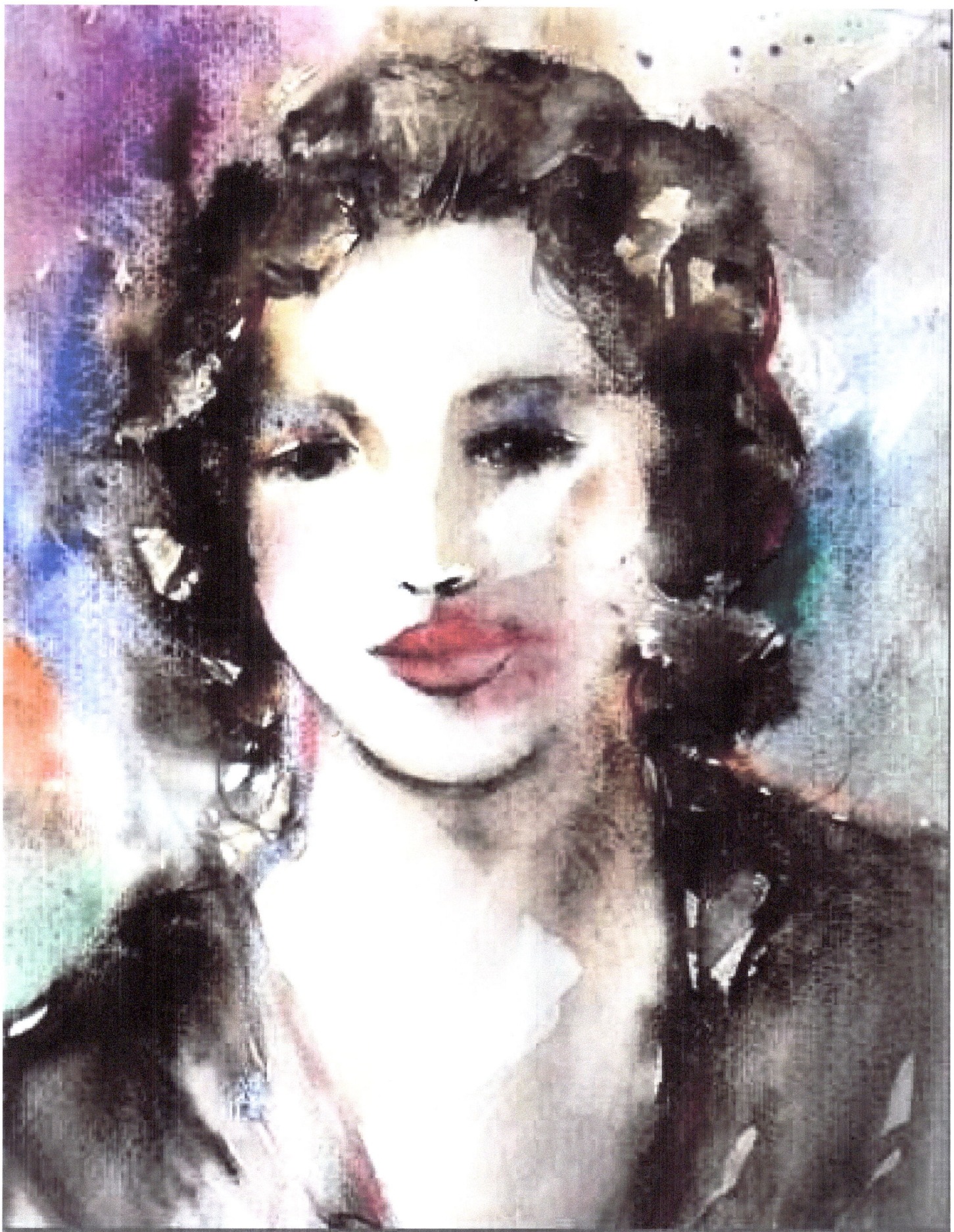

From Hermes Alegre Art Gallery Book-2

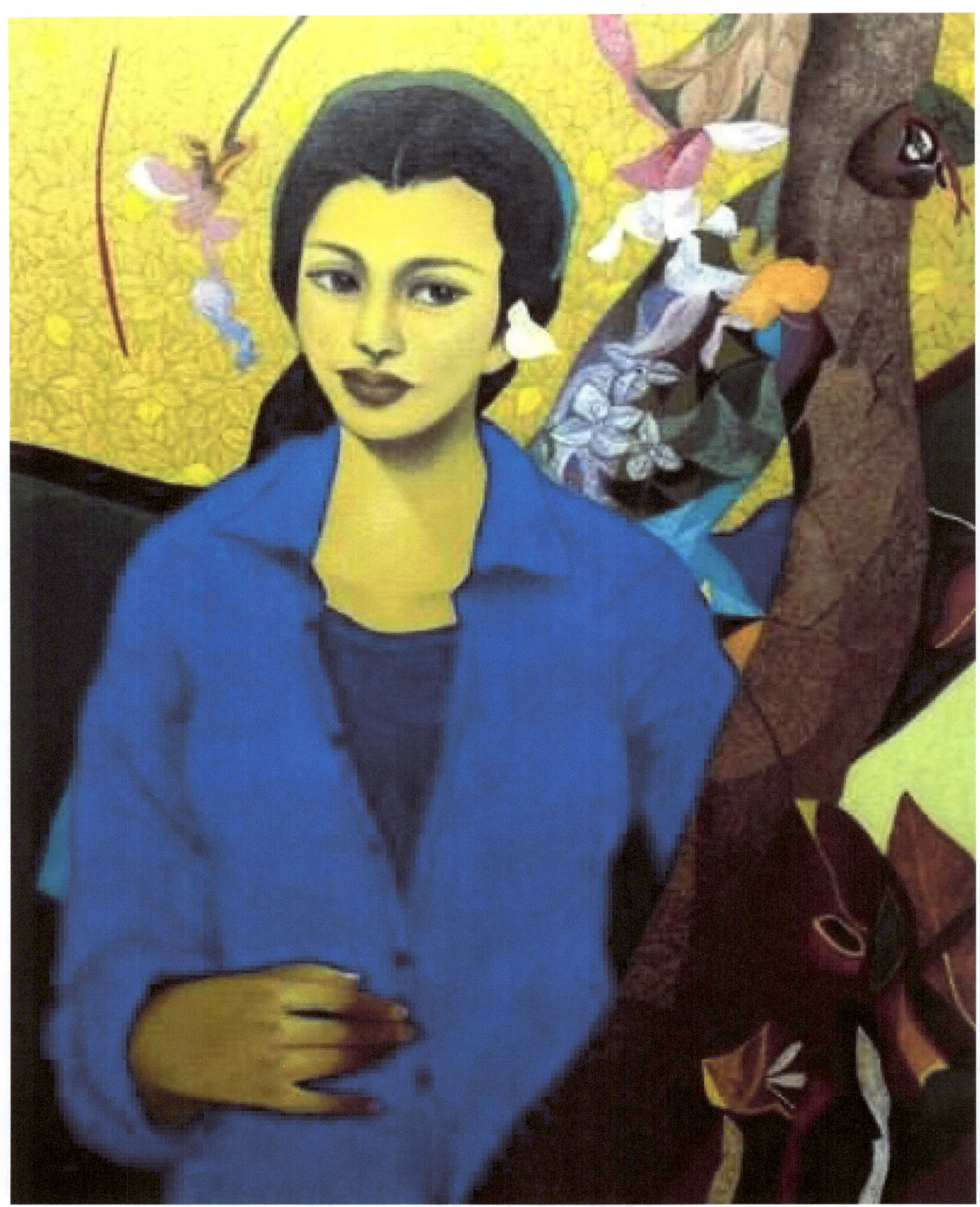

From Hermes Alegre Art Gallery Book-2

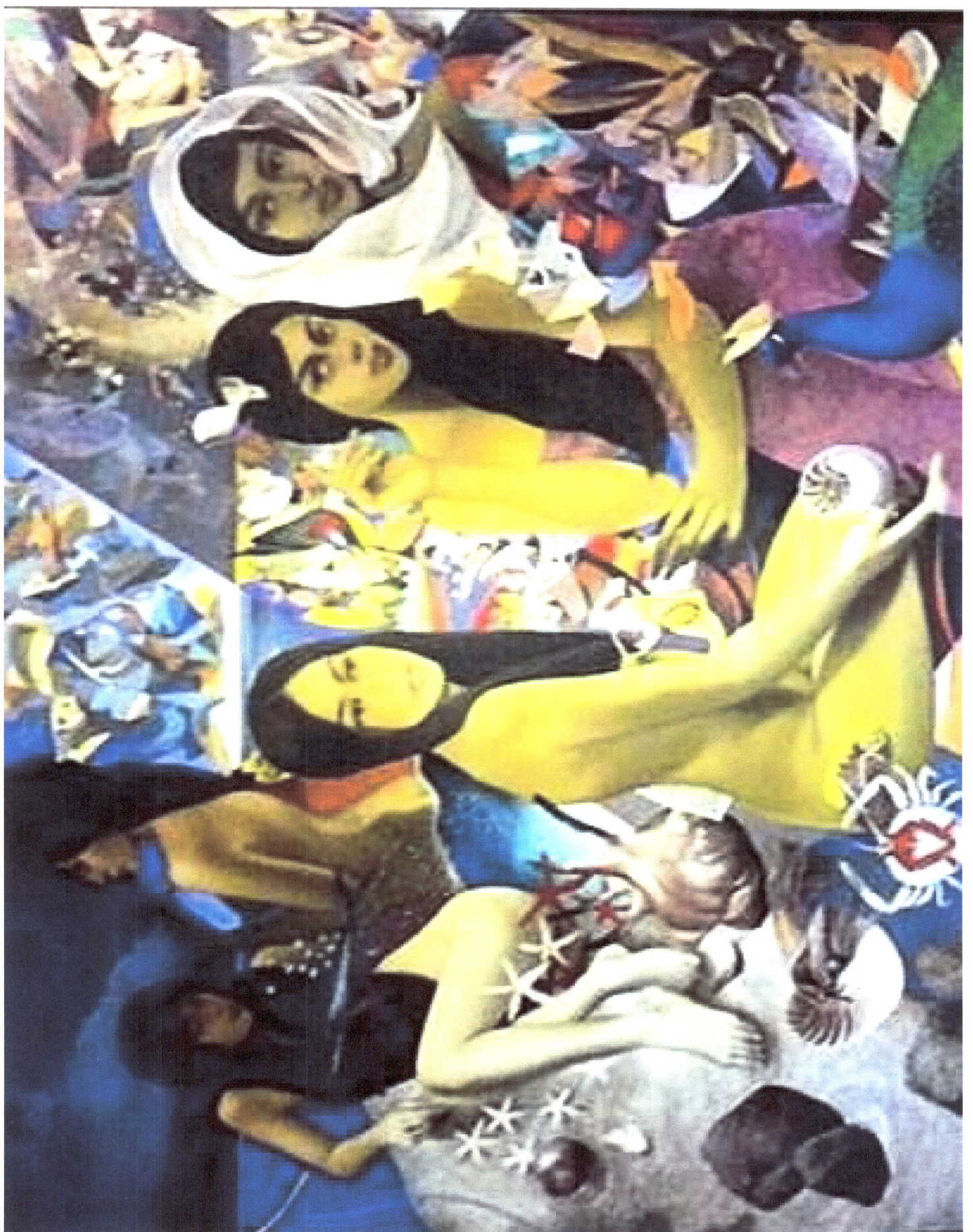

From Hermes Alegre Art Gallery Book-2

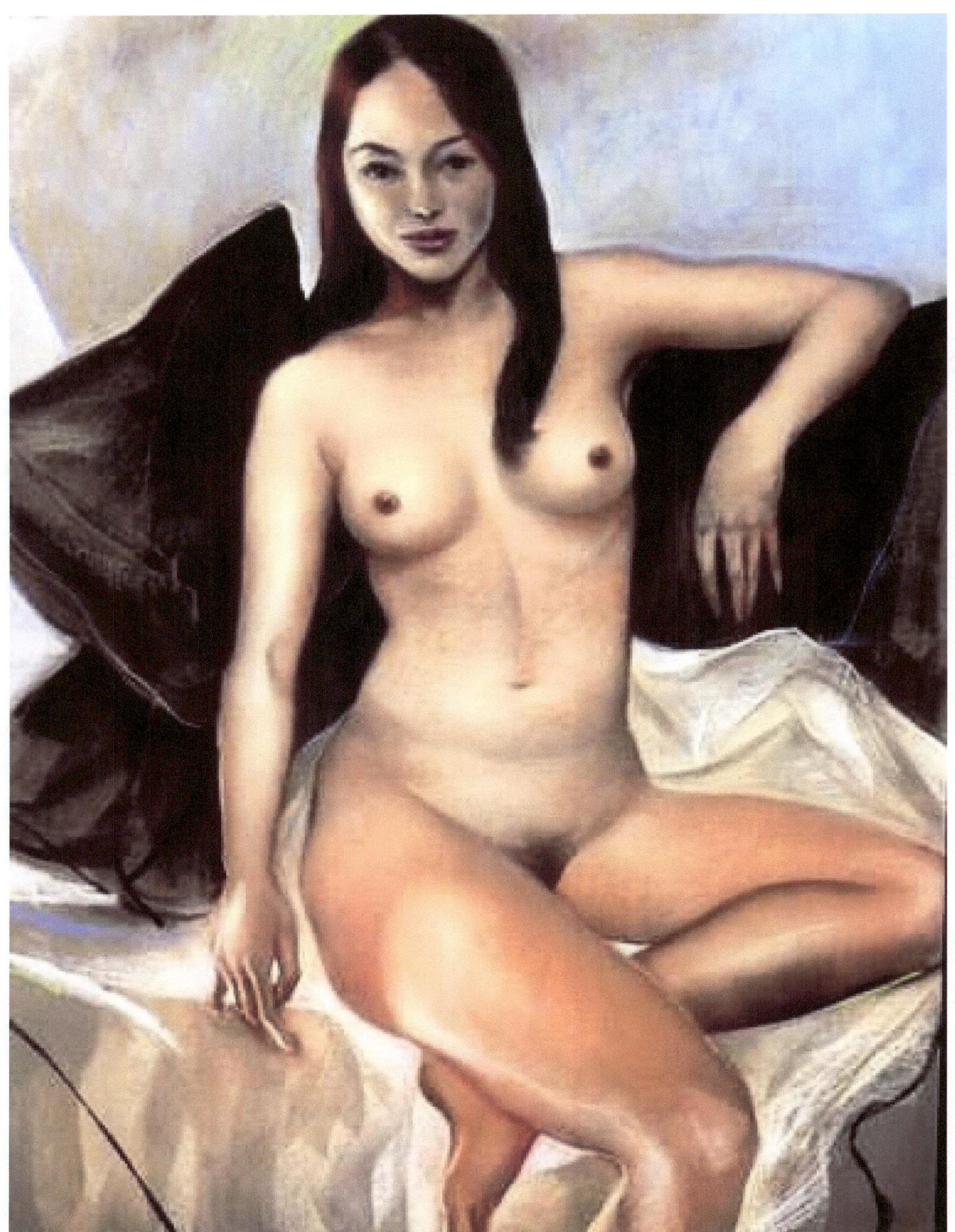

From Hermes Alegre Art Gallery Book-2

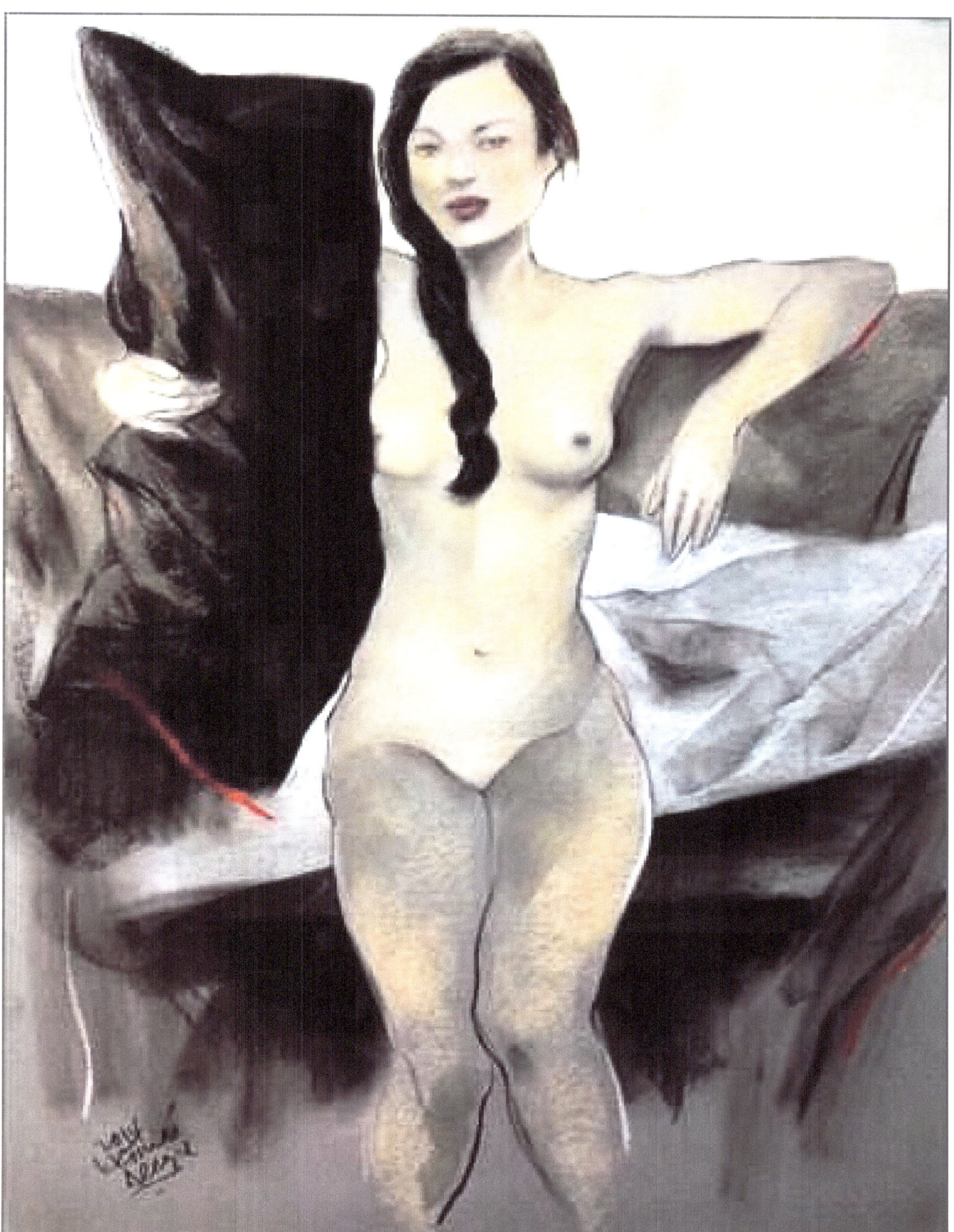

From Hermes Alegre Art Gallery Book-2

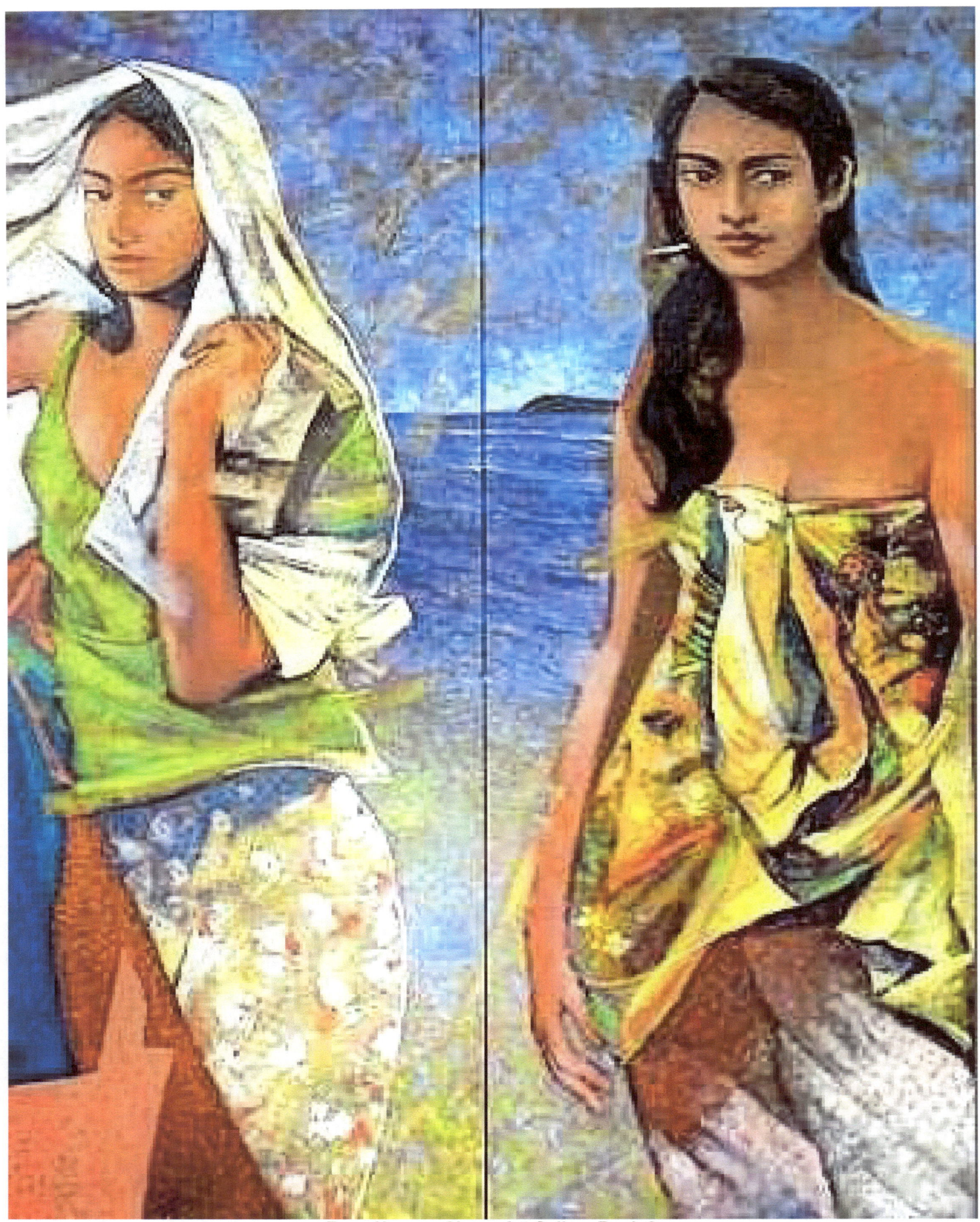

From Hermes Alegre Art Gallery Book-2

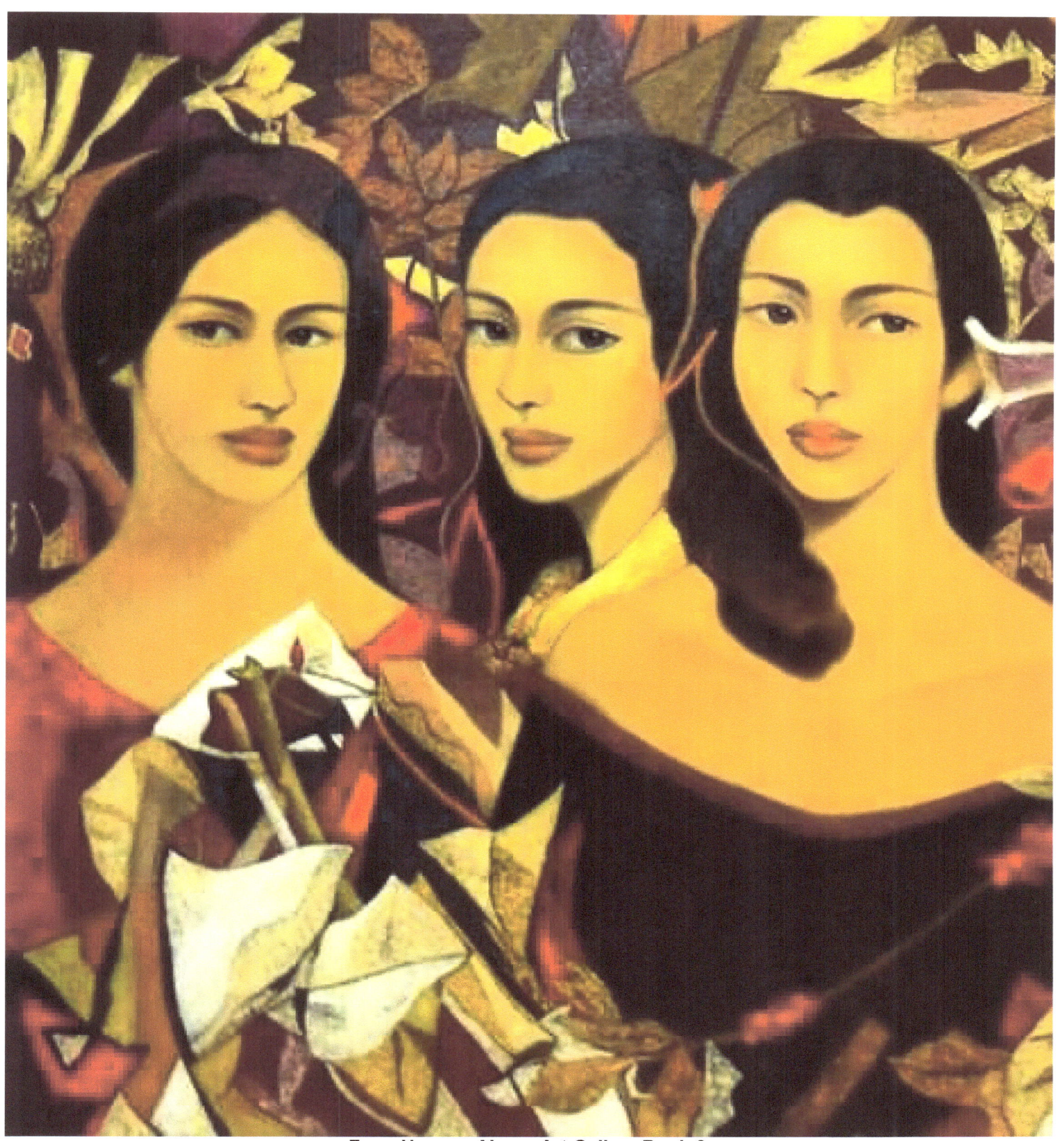

From Hermes Alegre Art Gallery Book-2

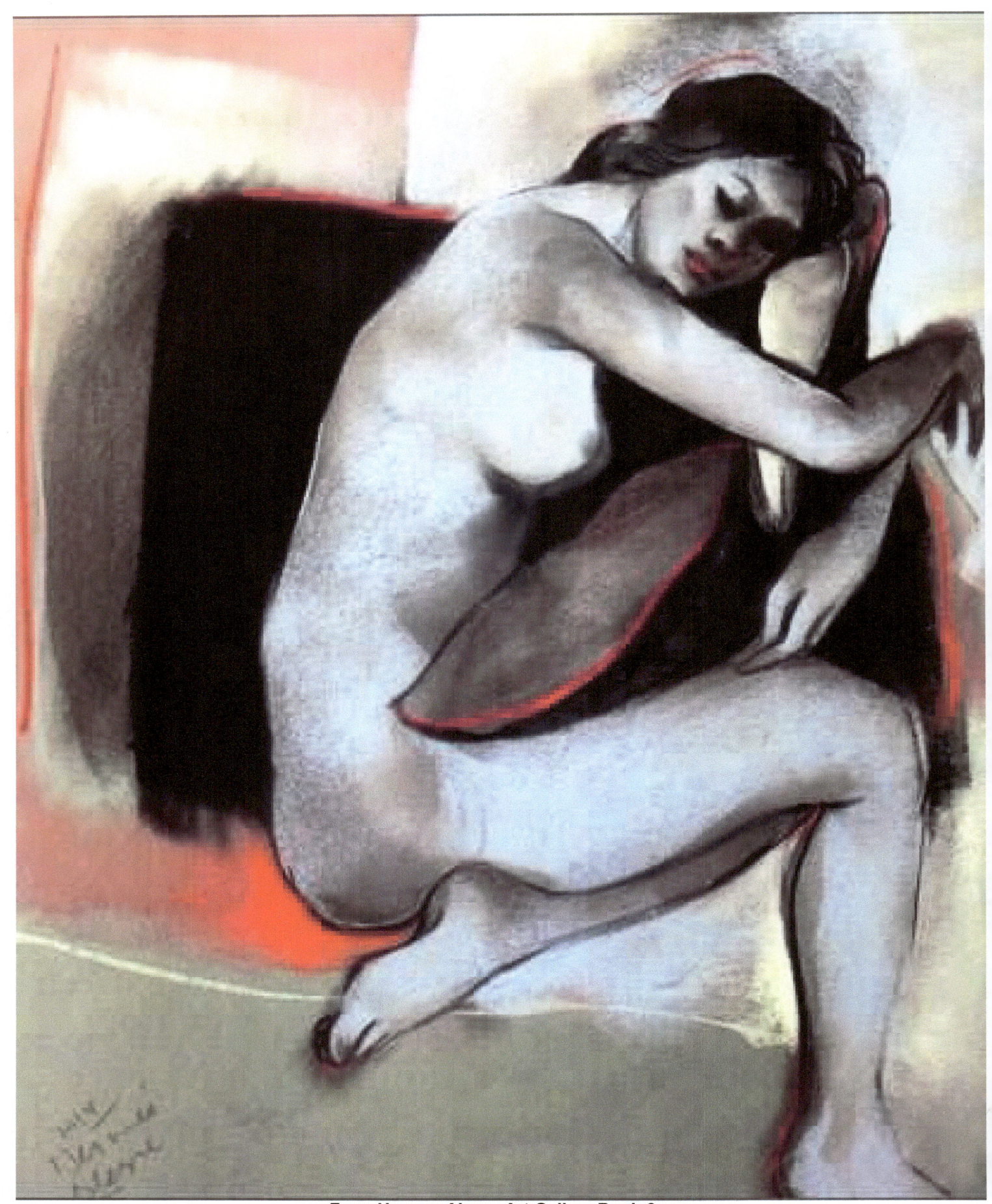

From Hermes Alegre Art Gallery Book-2

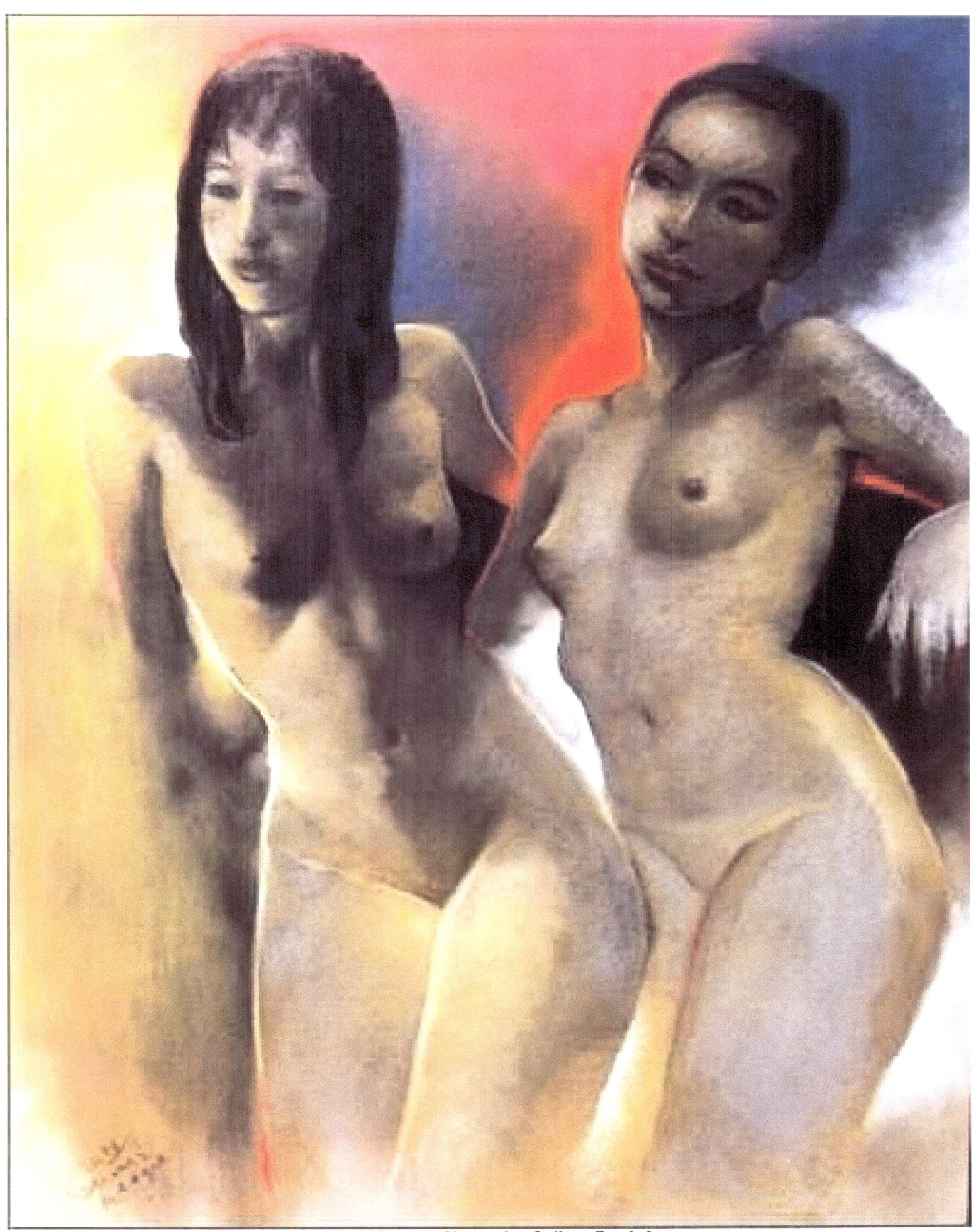

From Hermes Alegre Art Gallery Book-2

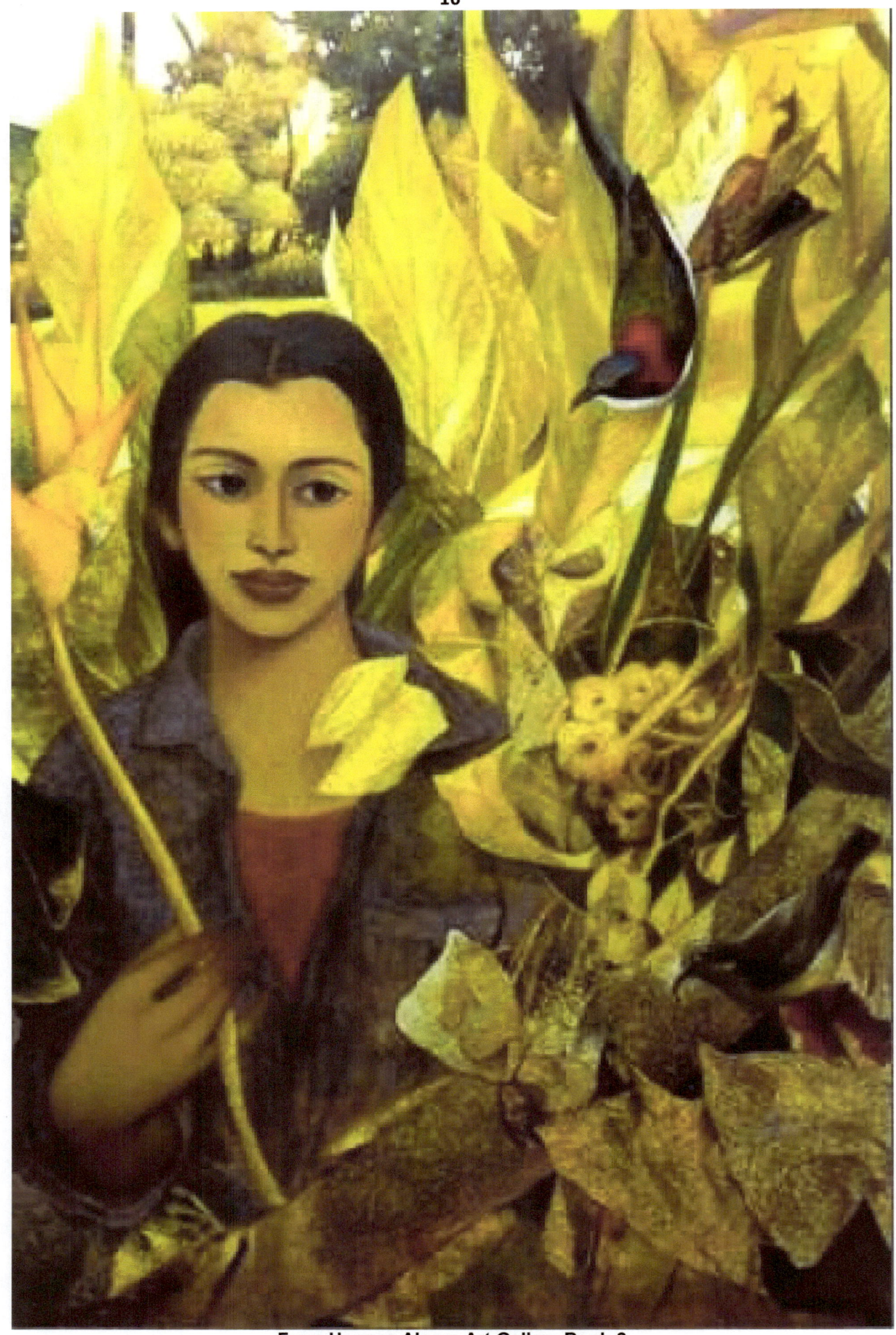

From Hermes Alegre Art Gallery Book-2

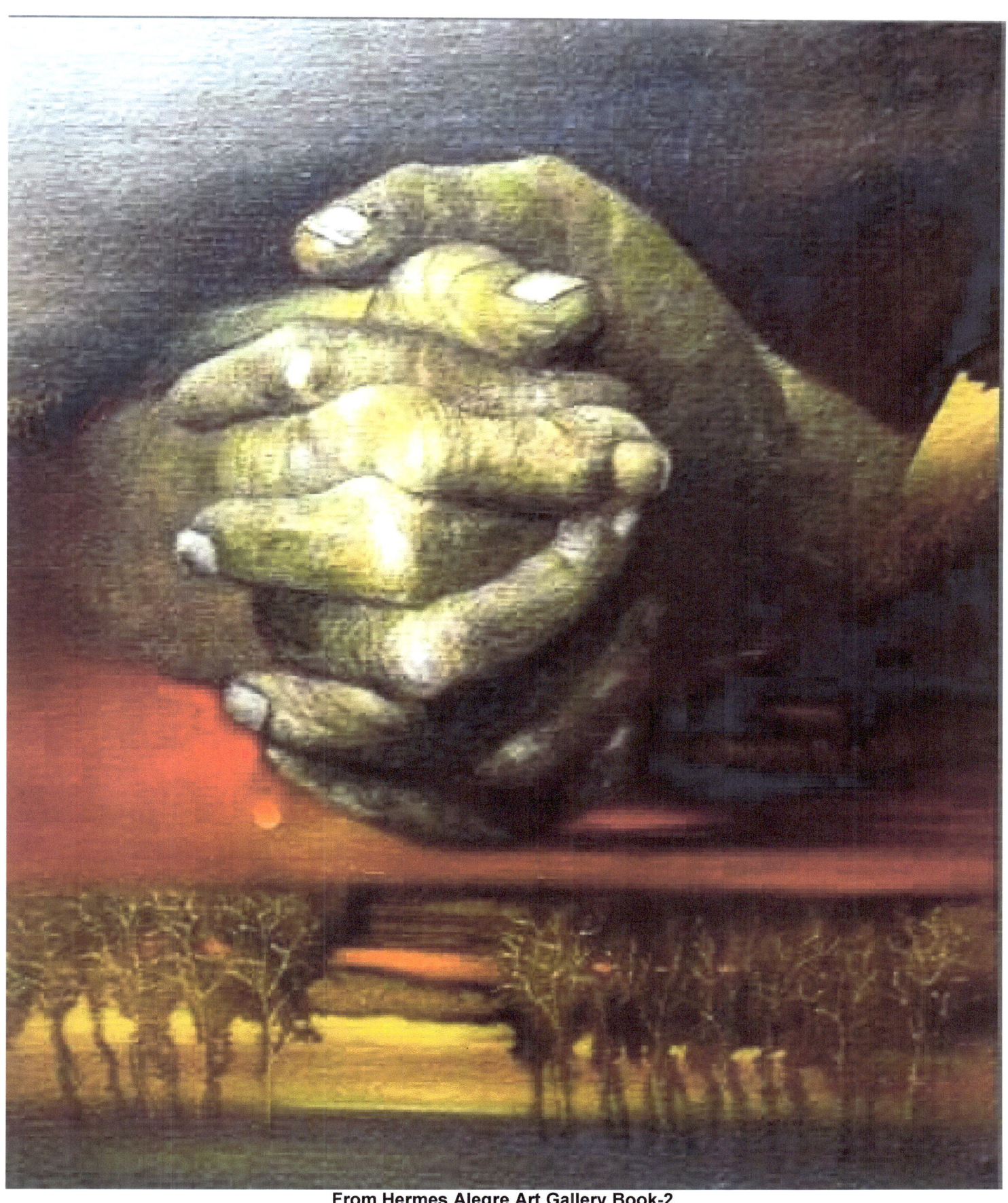

From Hermes Alegre Art Gallery Book-2

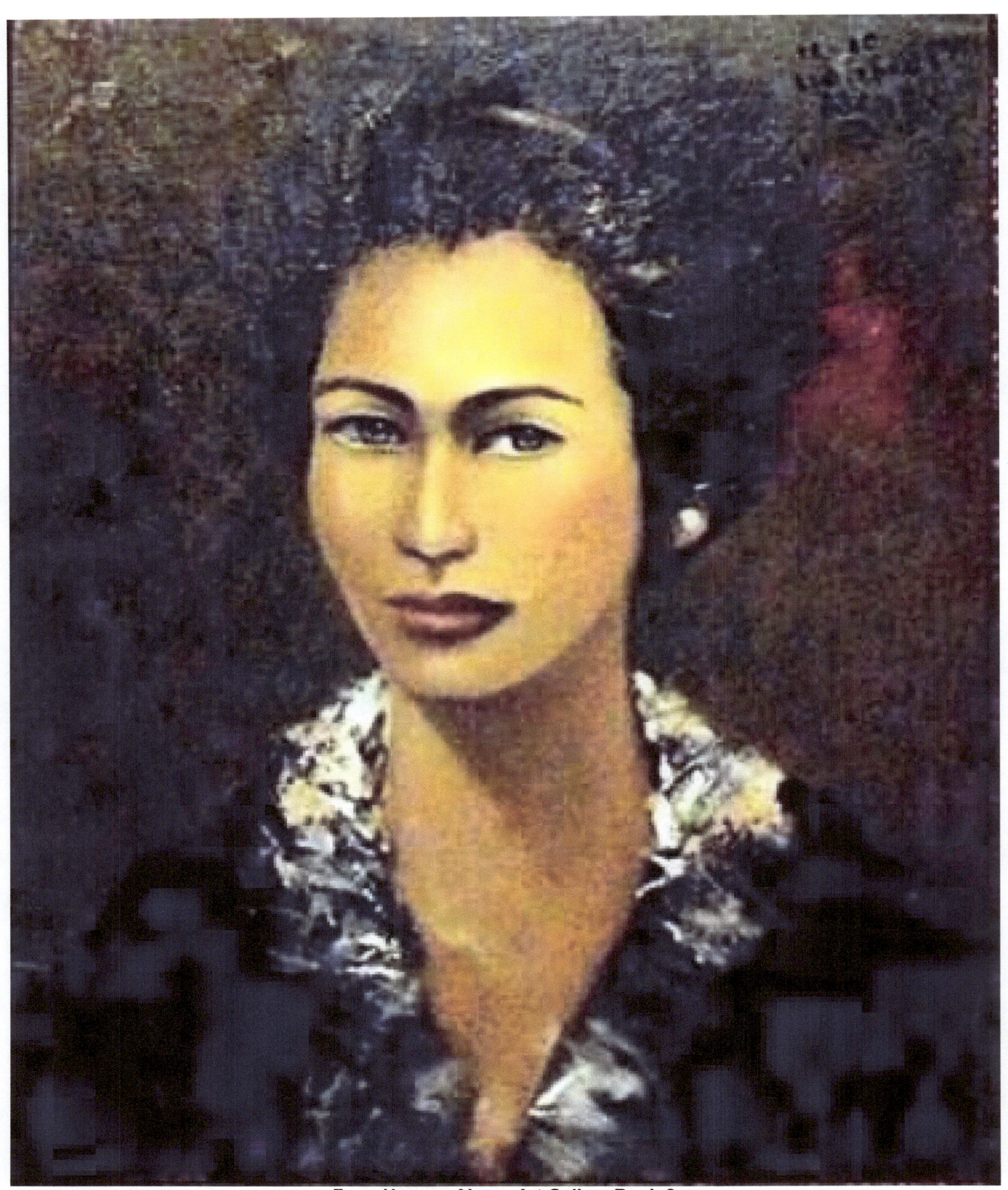

From Hermes Alegre Art Gallery Book-2

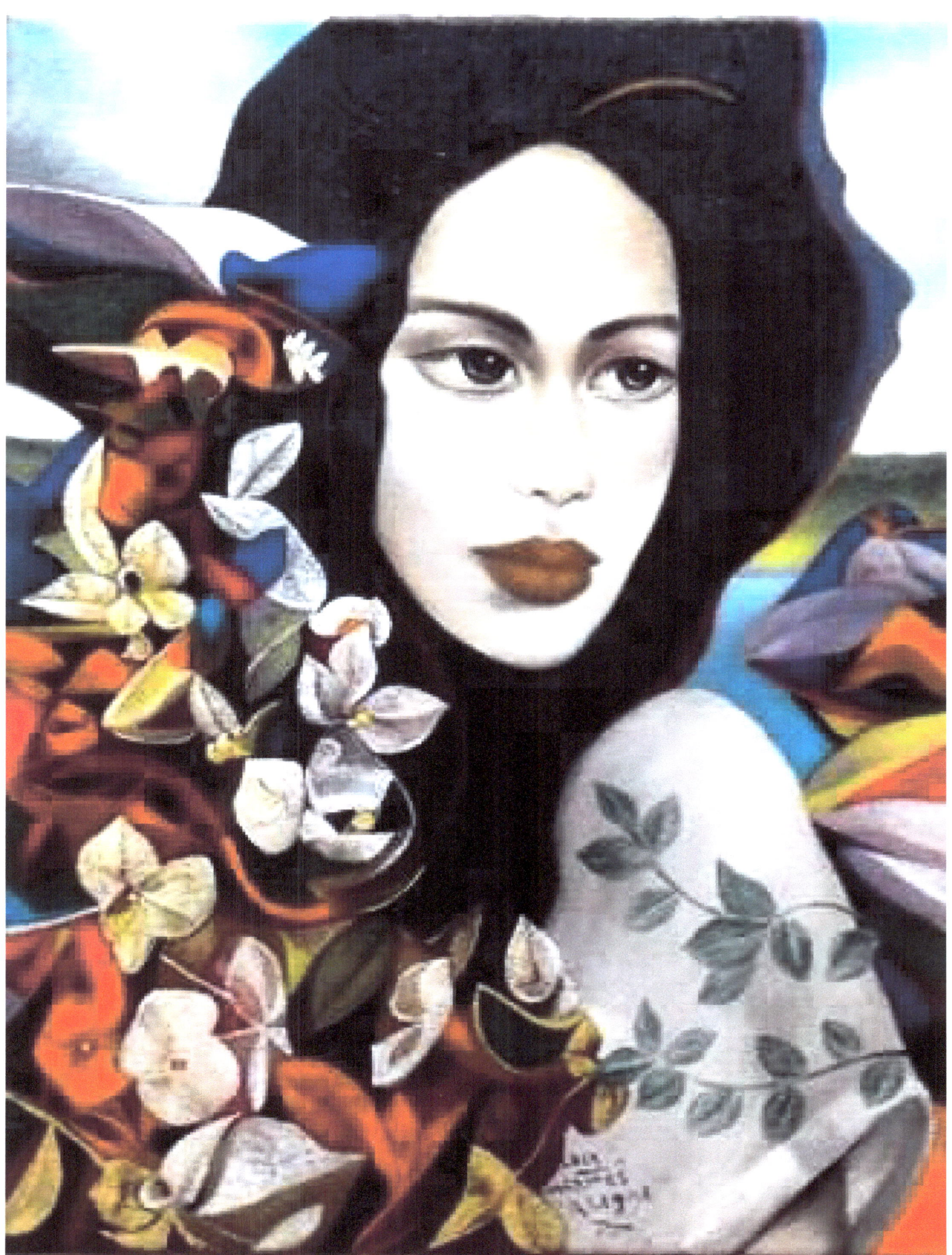

From Hermes Alegre Art Gallery Book-2

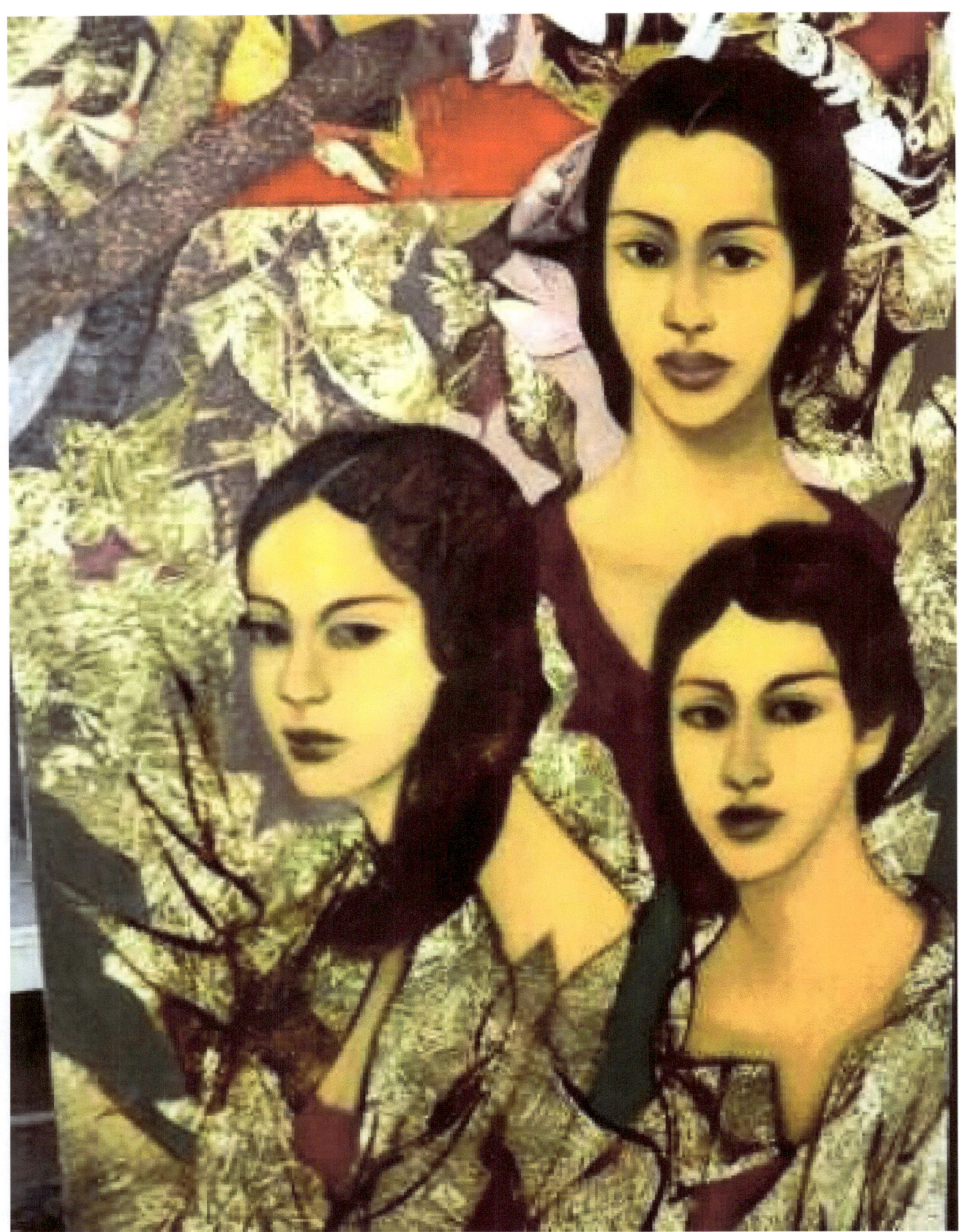

From Hermes Alegre Art Gallery Book-2

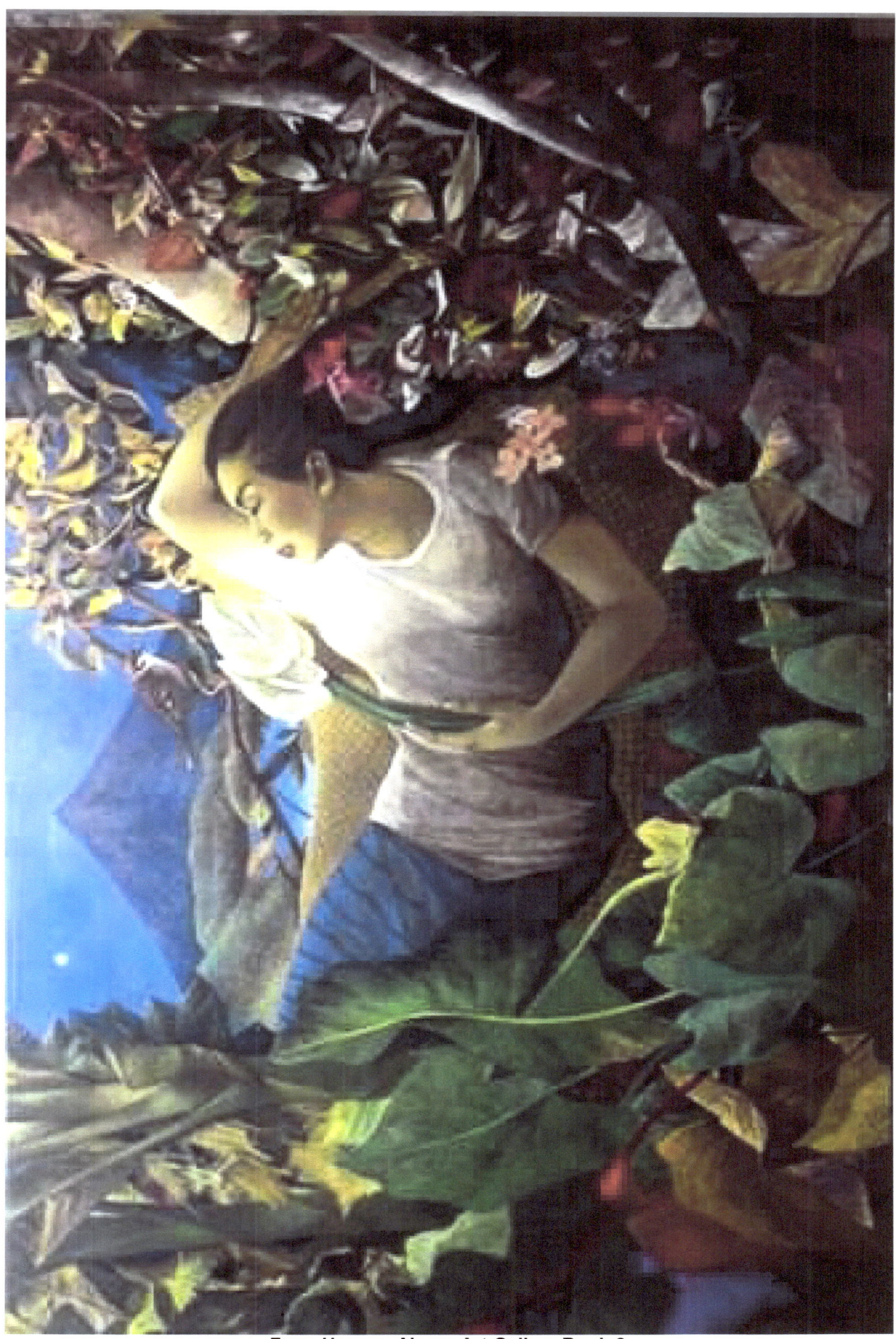

From Hermes Alegre Art Gallery Book-2

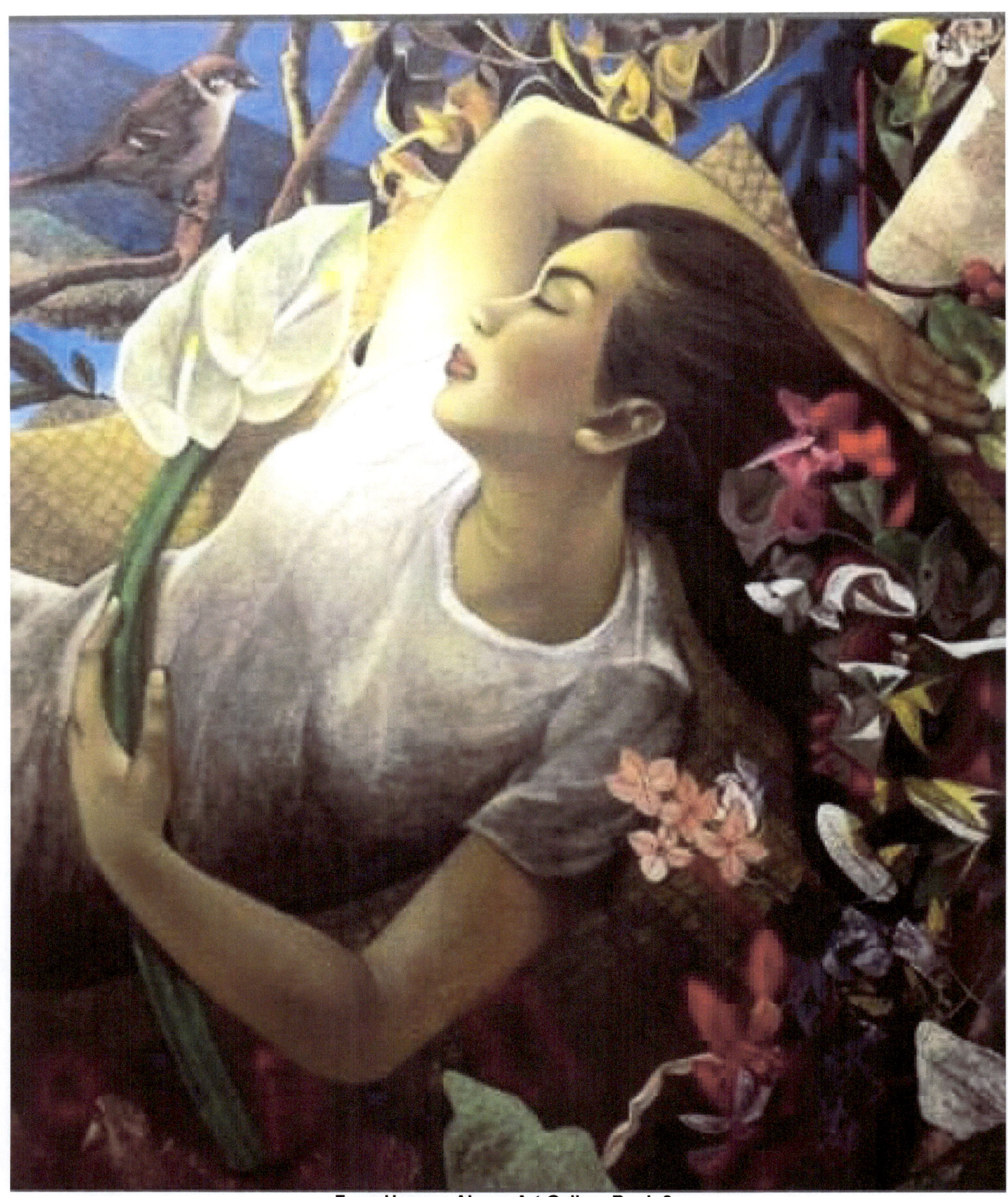

From Hermes Alegre Art Gallery Book-2

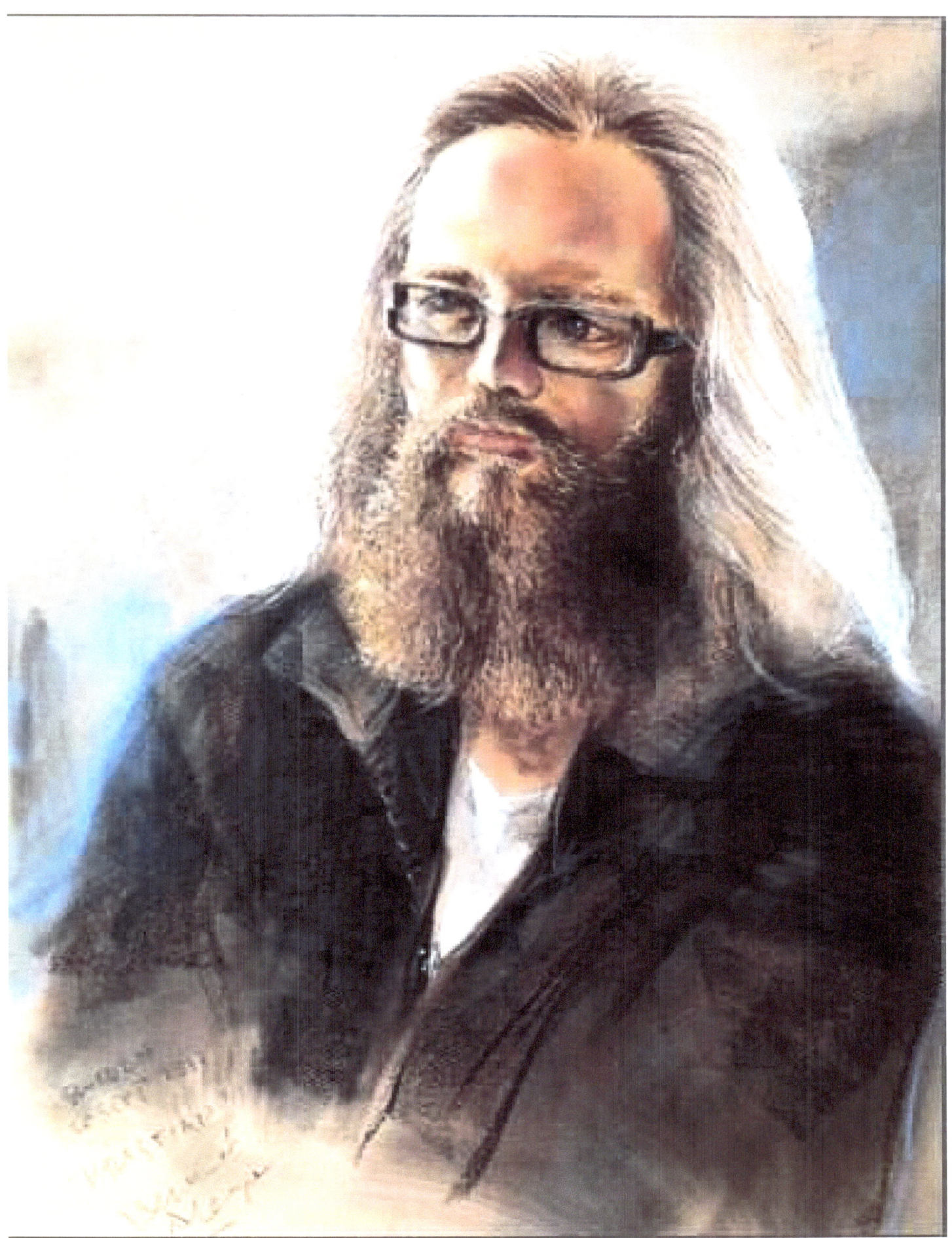

From Hermes Alegre Art Gallery Book-2

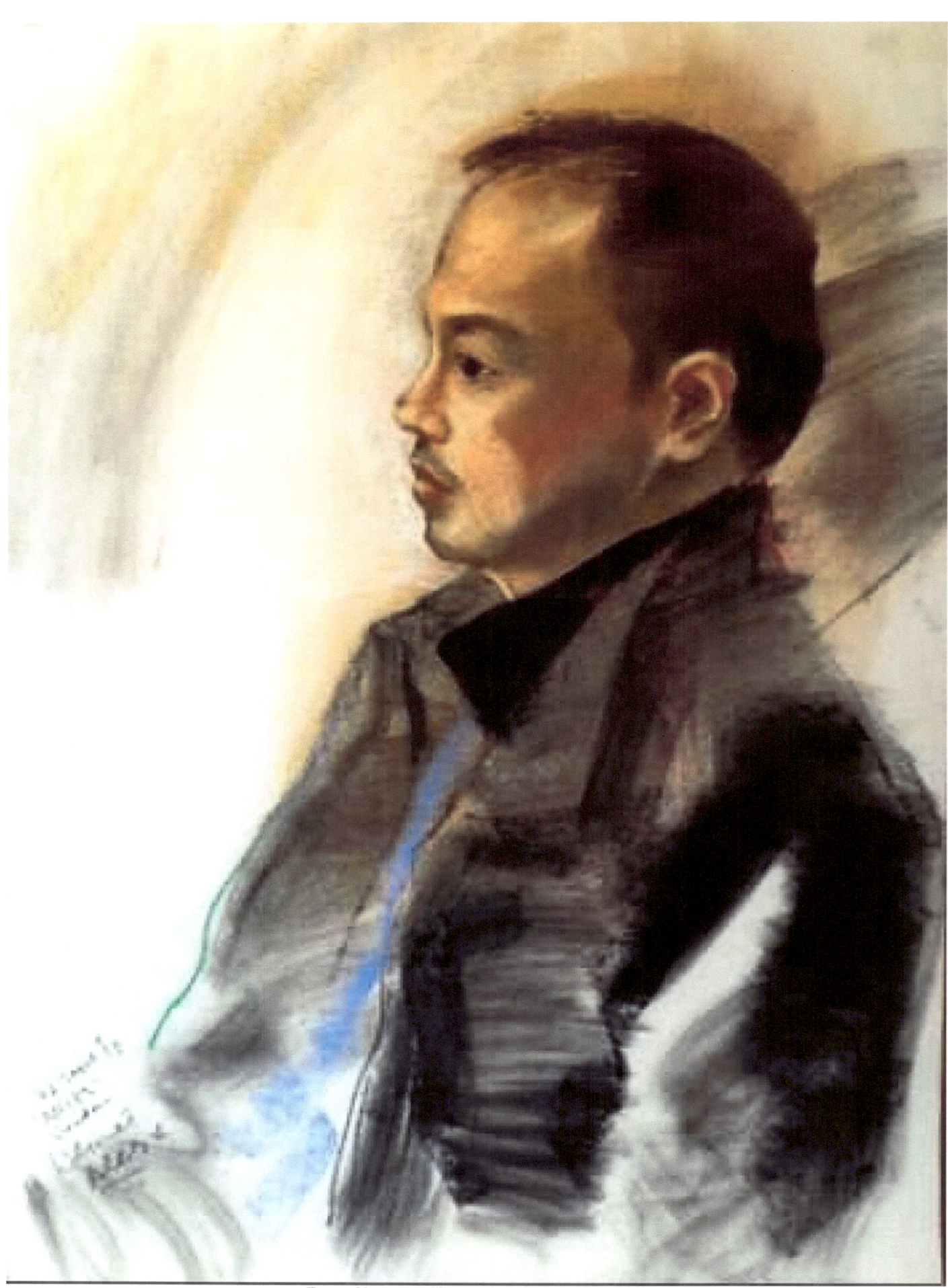

From Hermes Alegre Art Gallery Book-2

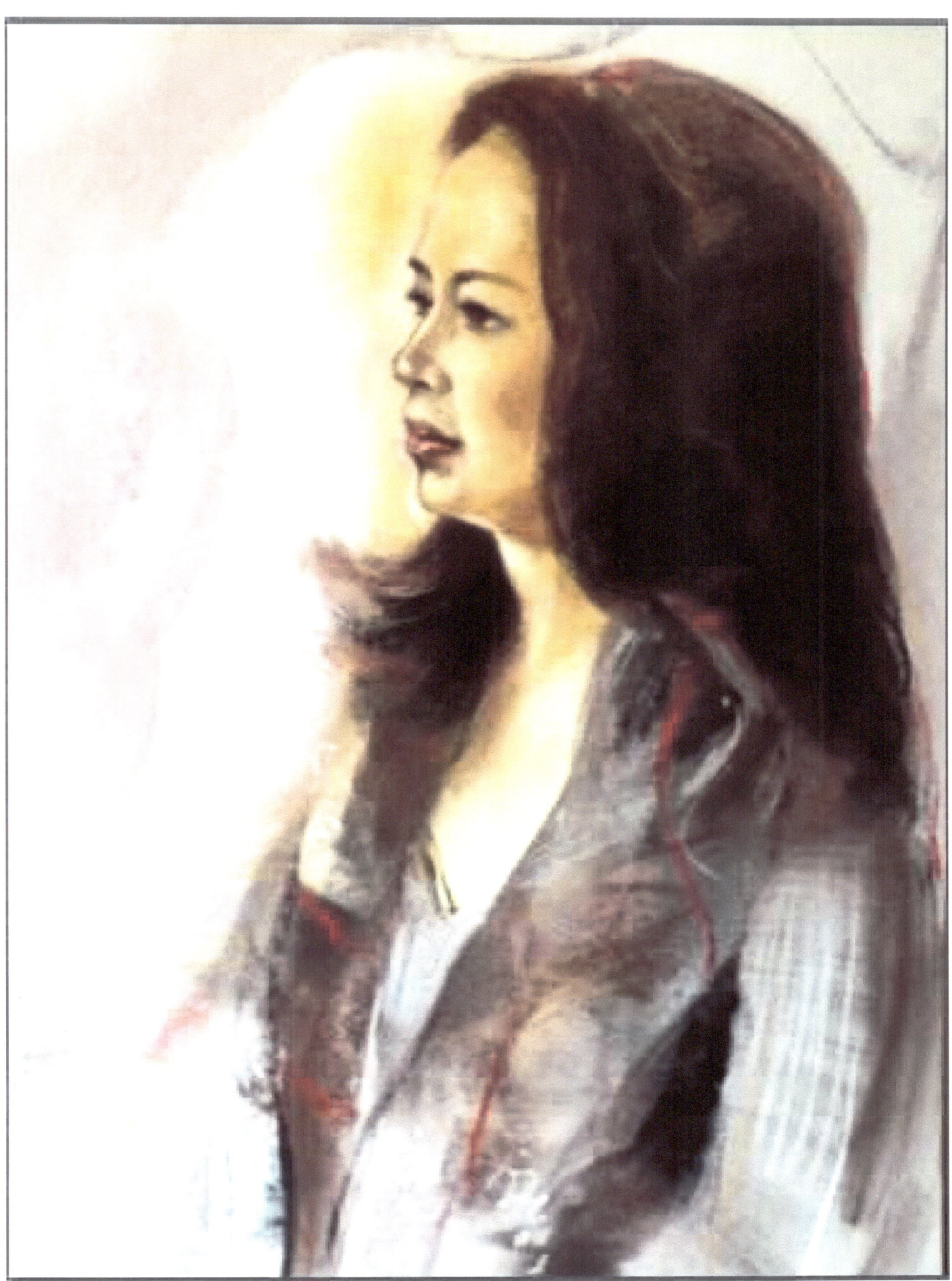

From Hermes Alegre Art Gallery Book-2

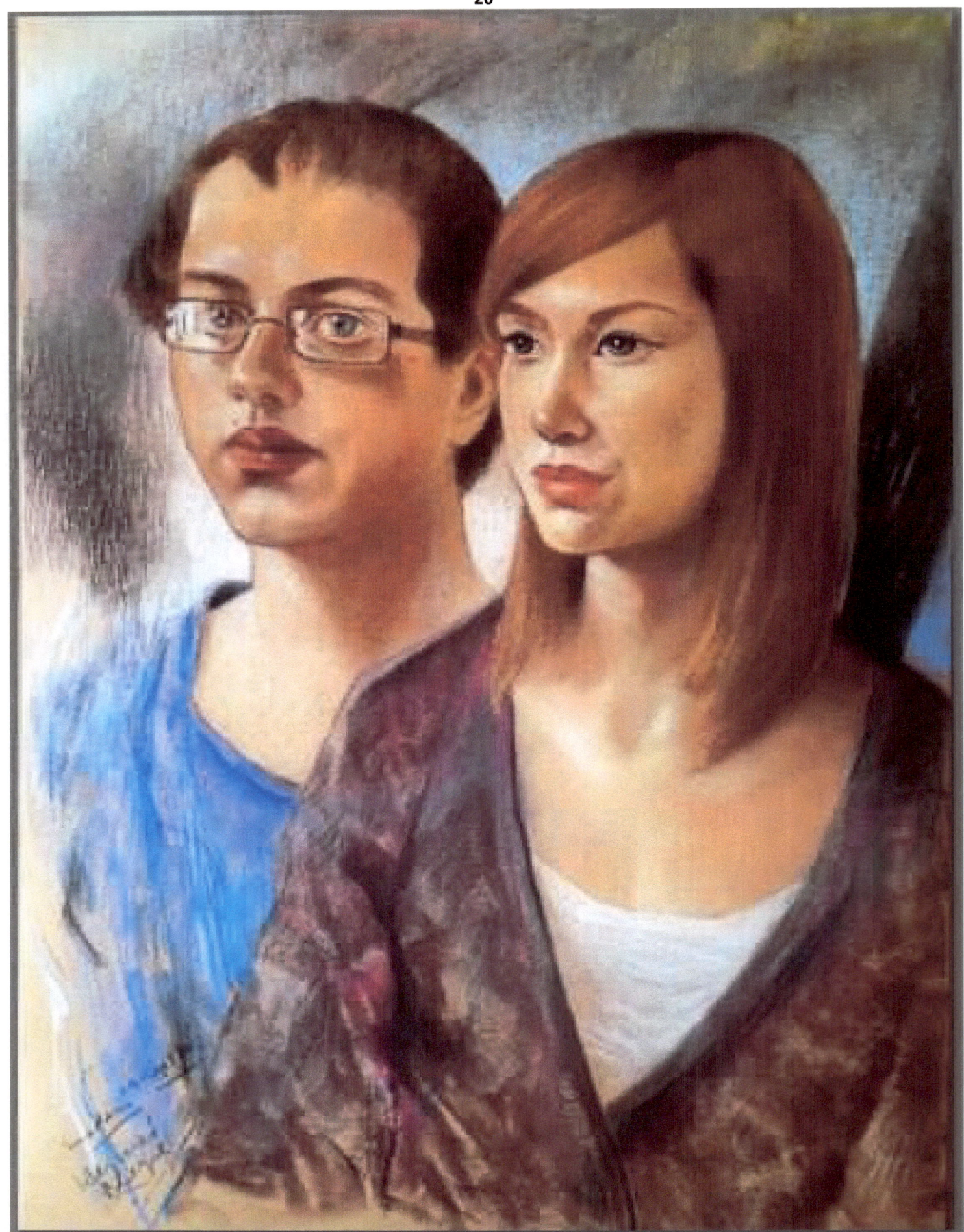

From Hermes Alegre Art Gallery Book-2

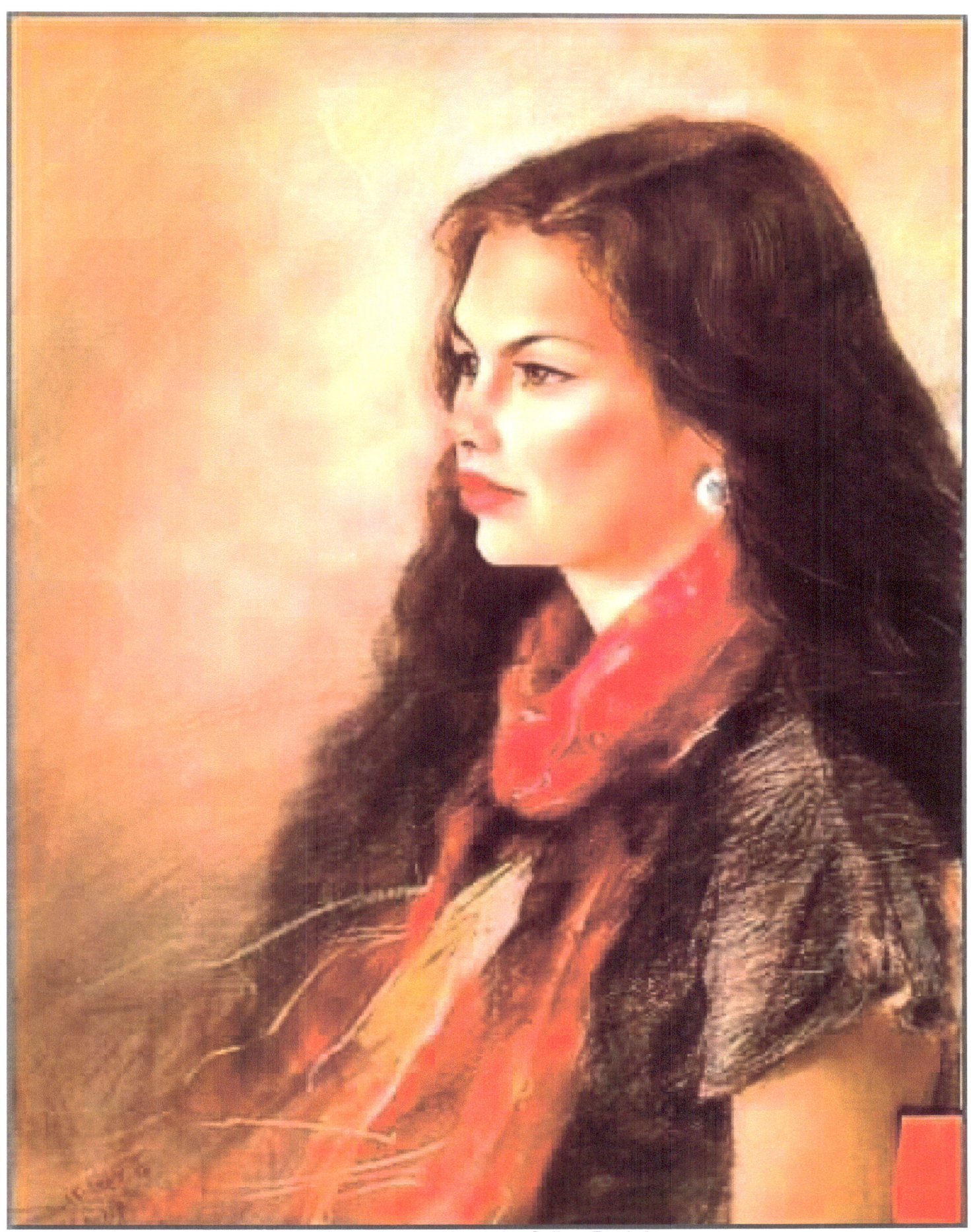

From Hermes Alegre Art Gallery Book-2

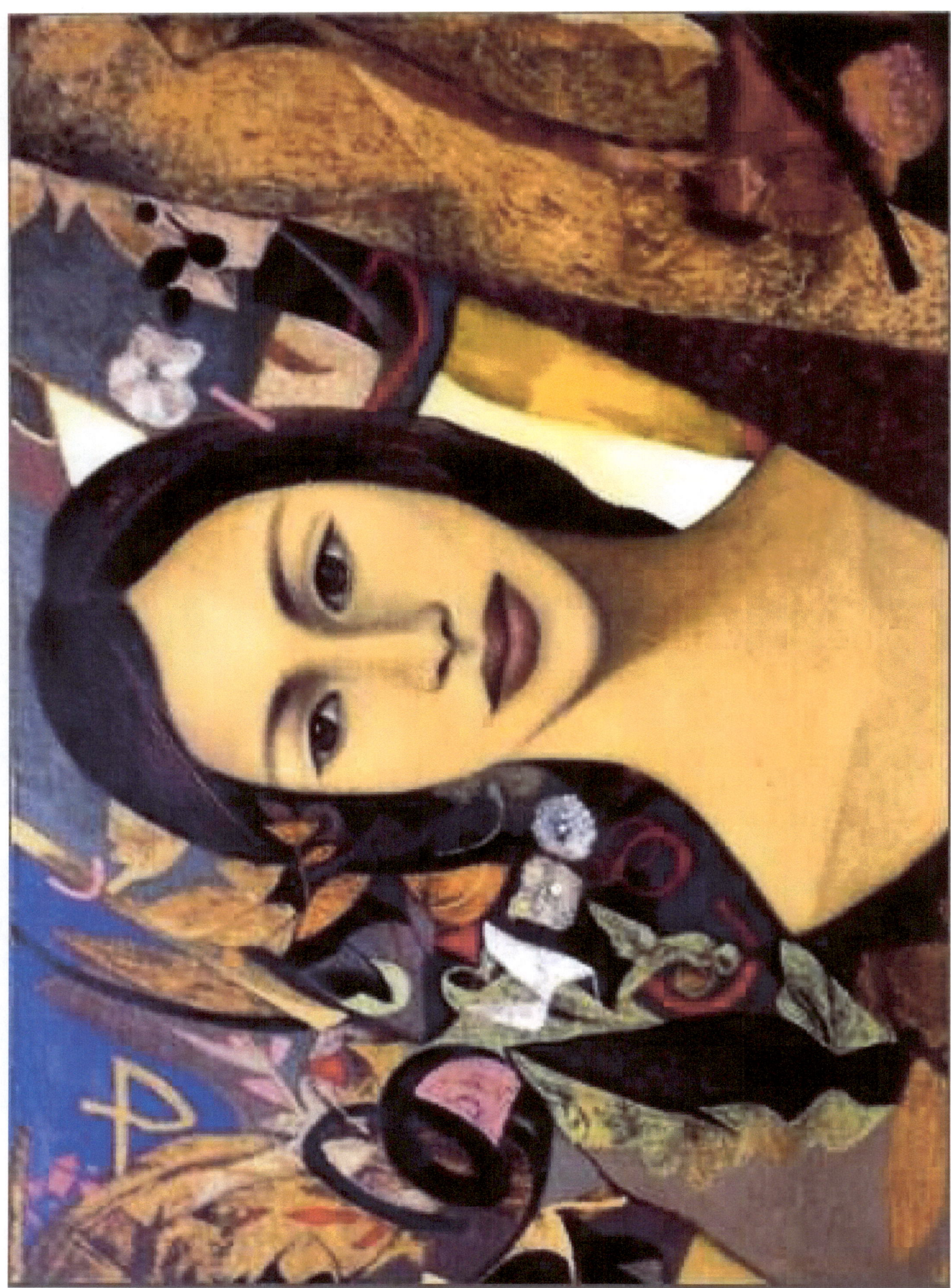

From Hermes Alegre Art Gallery Book-2

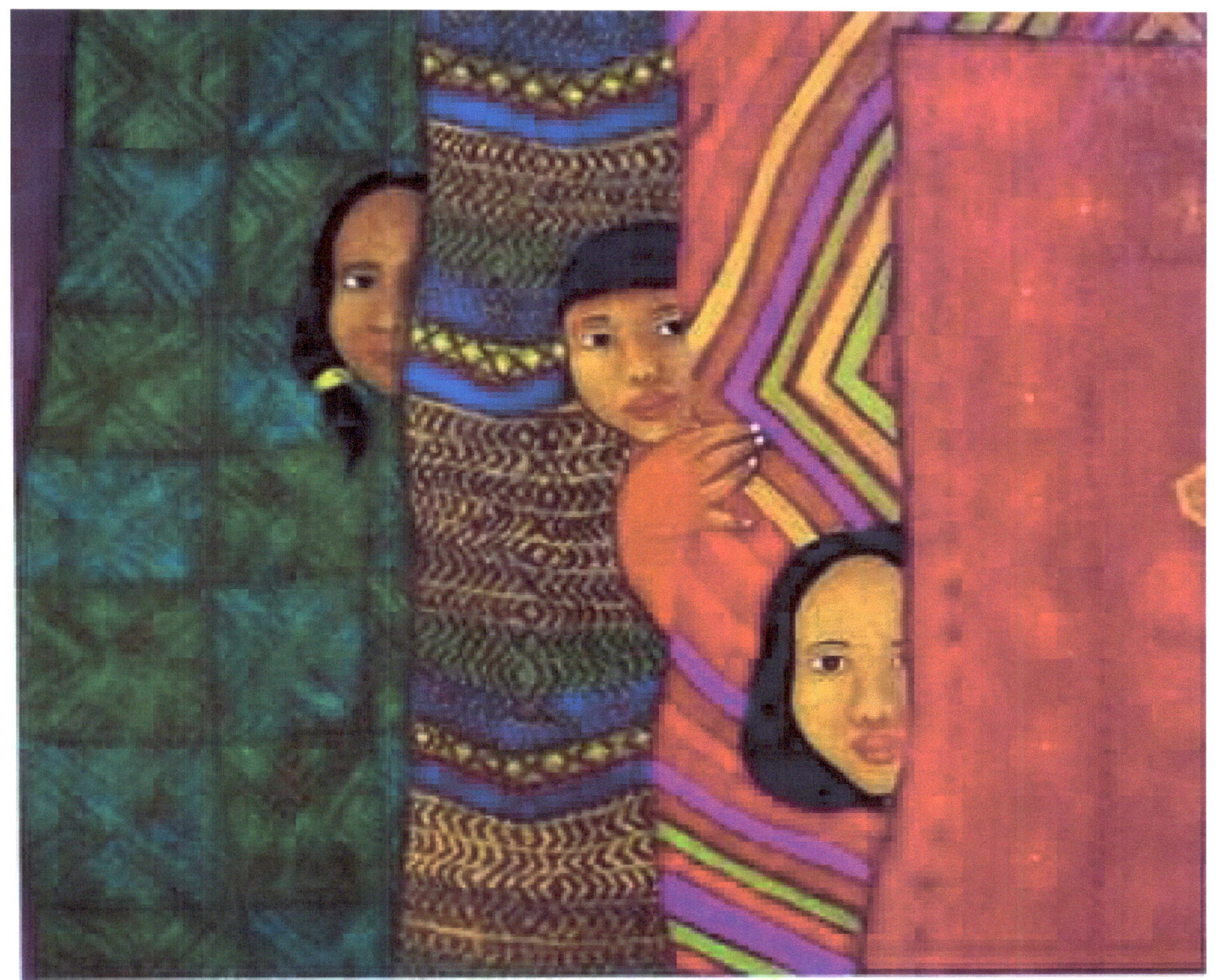

THE MATS

by Francisco Arcellana • illustrated by Hermes Alègre

From Hermes Alegre Art Gallery Book-2

Welcome to Hermes Alegre Art Gallery Book-2, size 8.5x11. Hermes hails from Daet, Camarines Norte and has created great excitement in the art world with his wonderful paintings for more than 20 years.

He finished his Art degree from PWU in Manila. His latest art show was done in NY City in mid 2011, together with his fellow artists. The purpose of this art book is to maximize exposure of his art work. Please contact his face book account under his name in case you are interested to order his works or commission him to paint for you. Copies of this book are available online and via self-publisher.

Due to his many paintings, hopefully further sequels of this book will be made. You can frame any of the paintings and hang them in walls, by buying extra copies of this book, which is very affordable

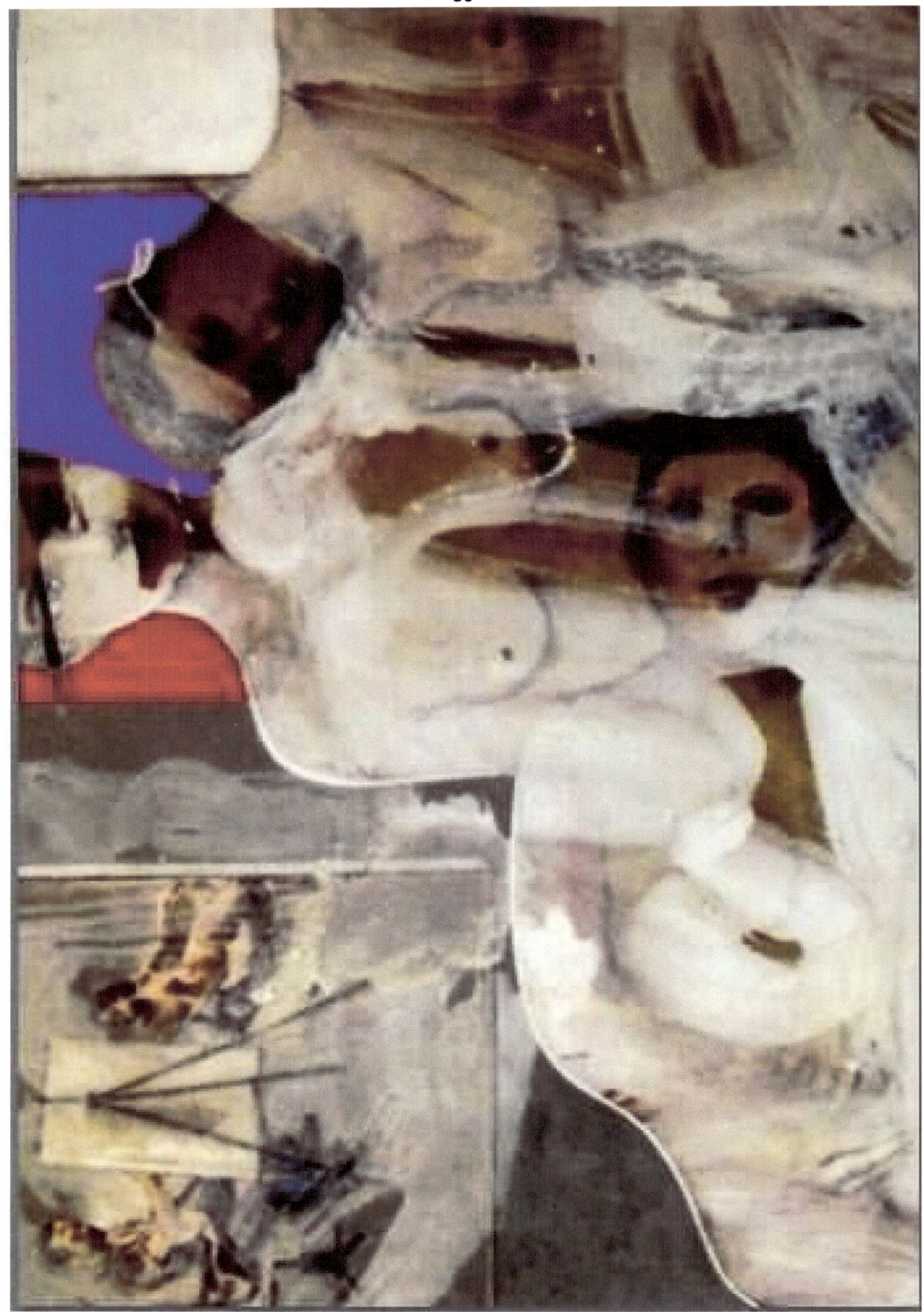

From Hermes Alegre Art Gallery Book-2

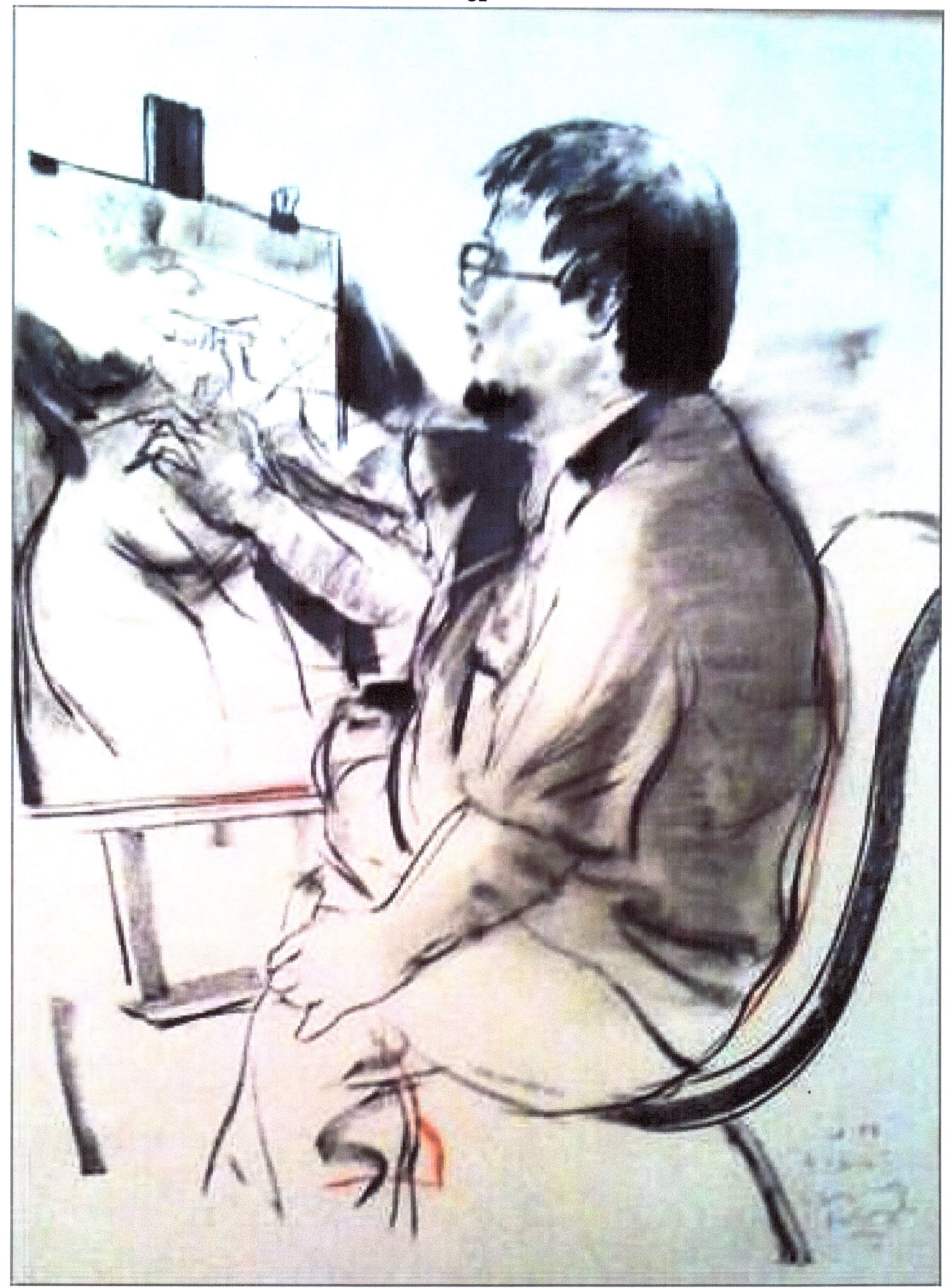

From Hermes Alegre Art Gallery Book-2

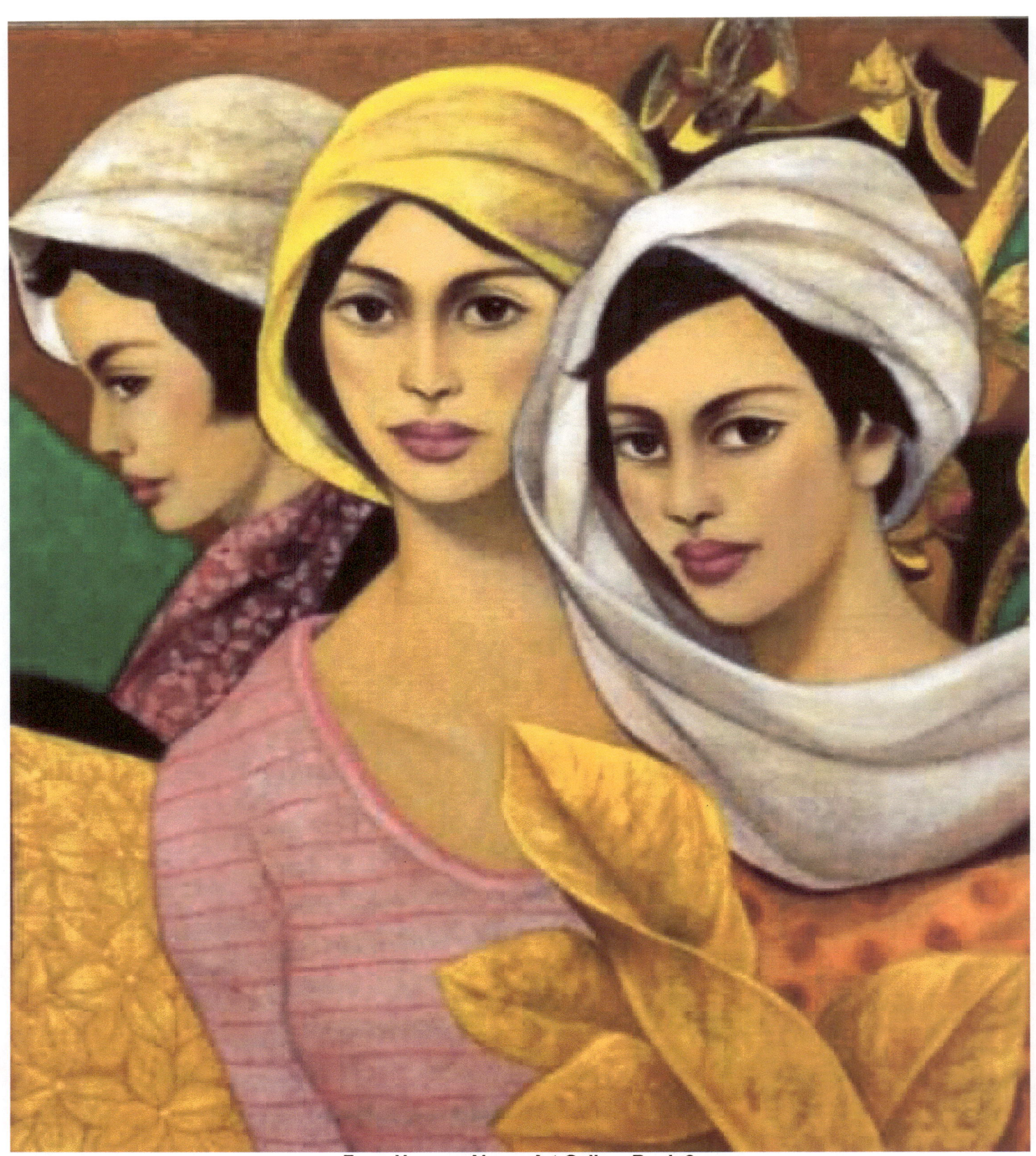

From Hermes Alegre Art Gallery Book-2

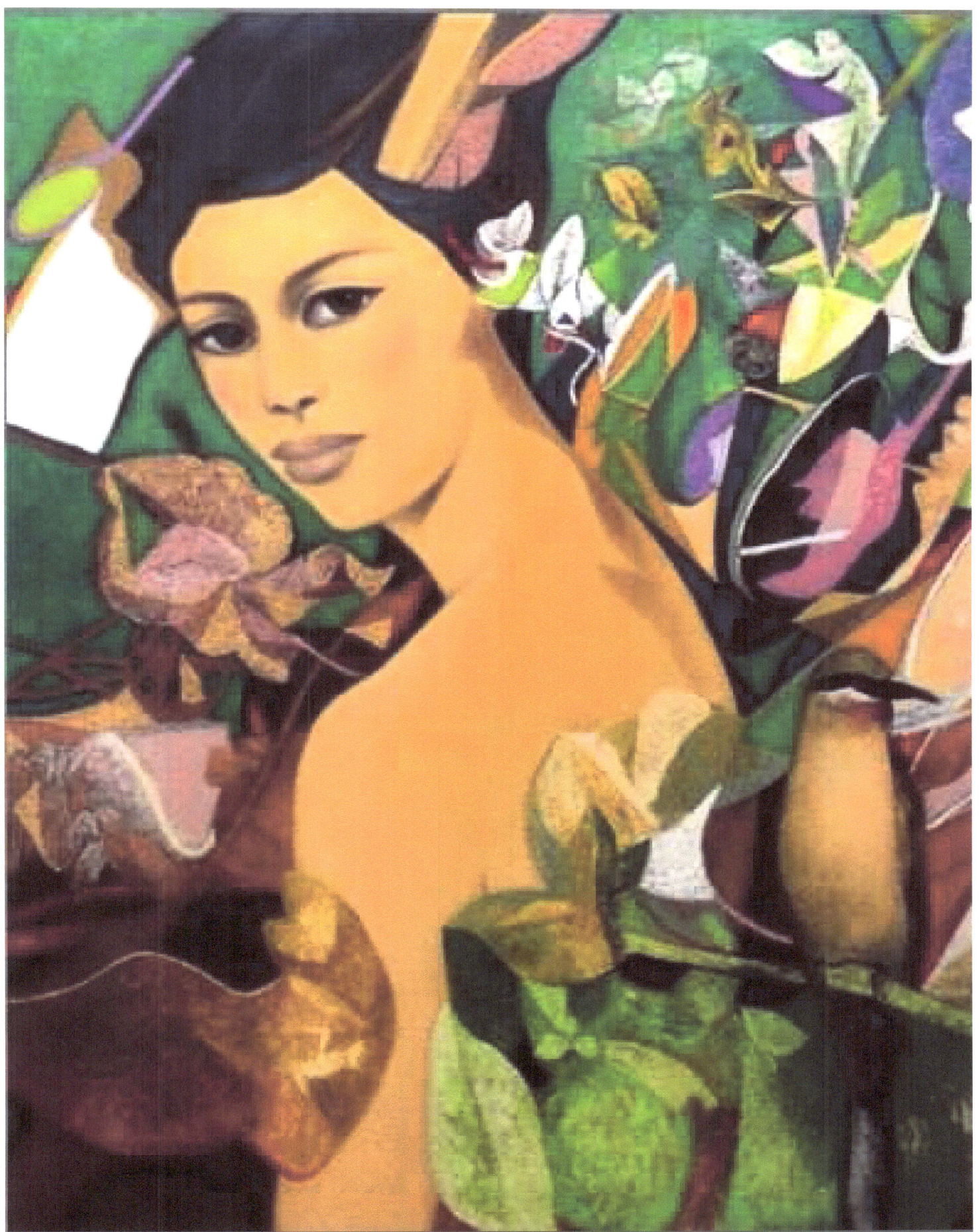

From Hermes Alegre Art Gallery Book-2

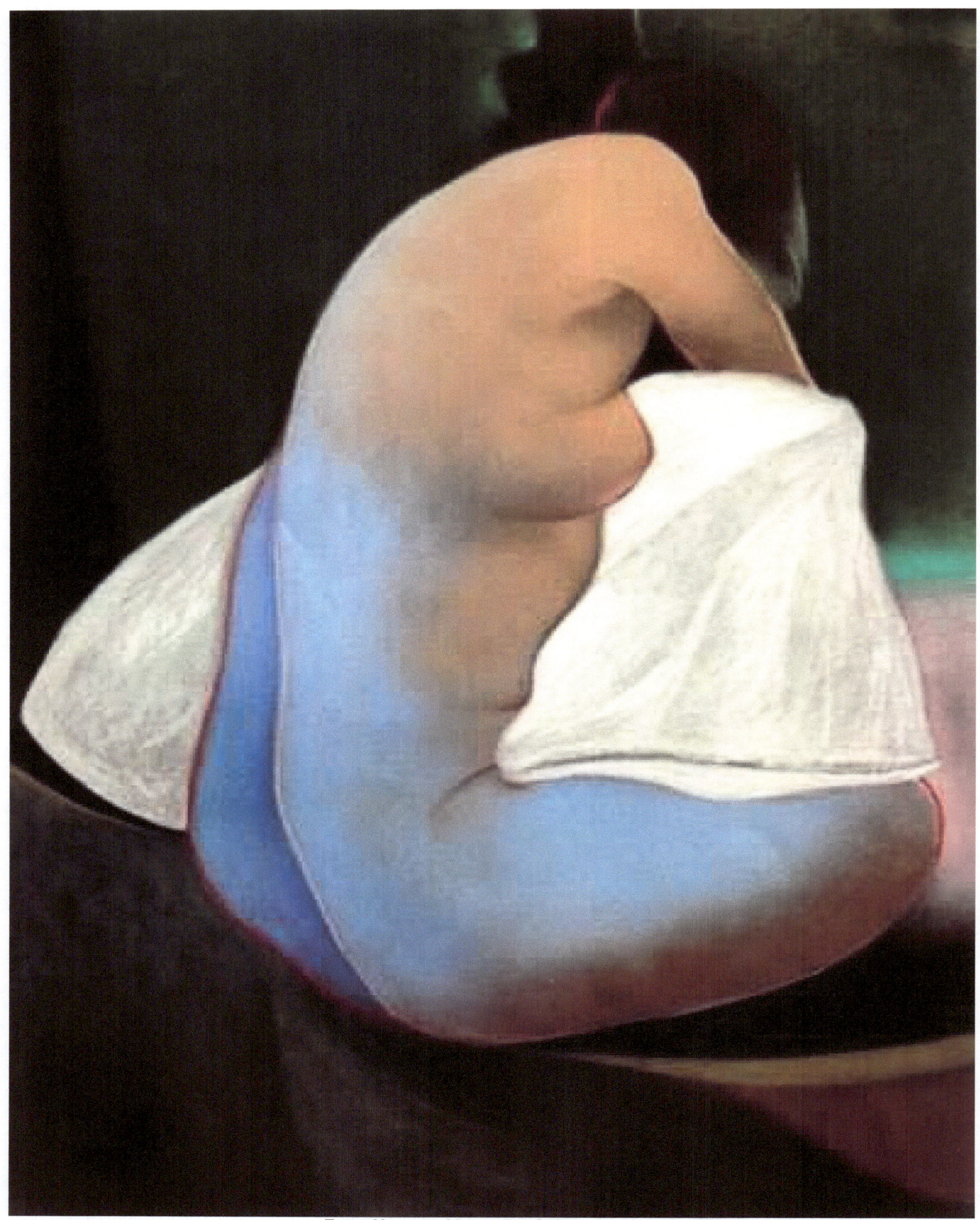

From Hermes Alegre Art Gallery Book-2

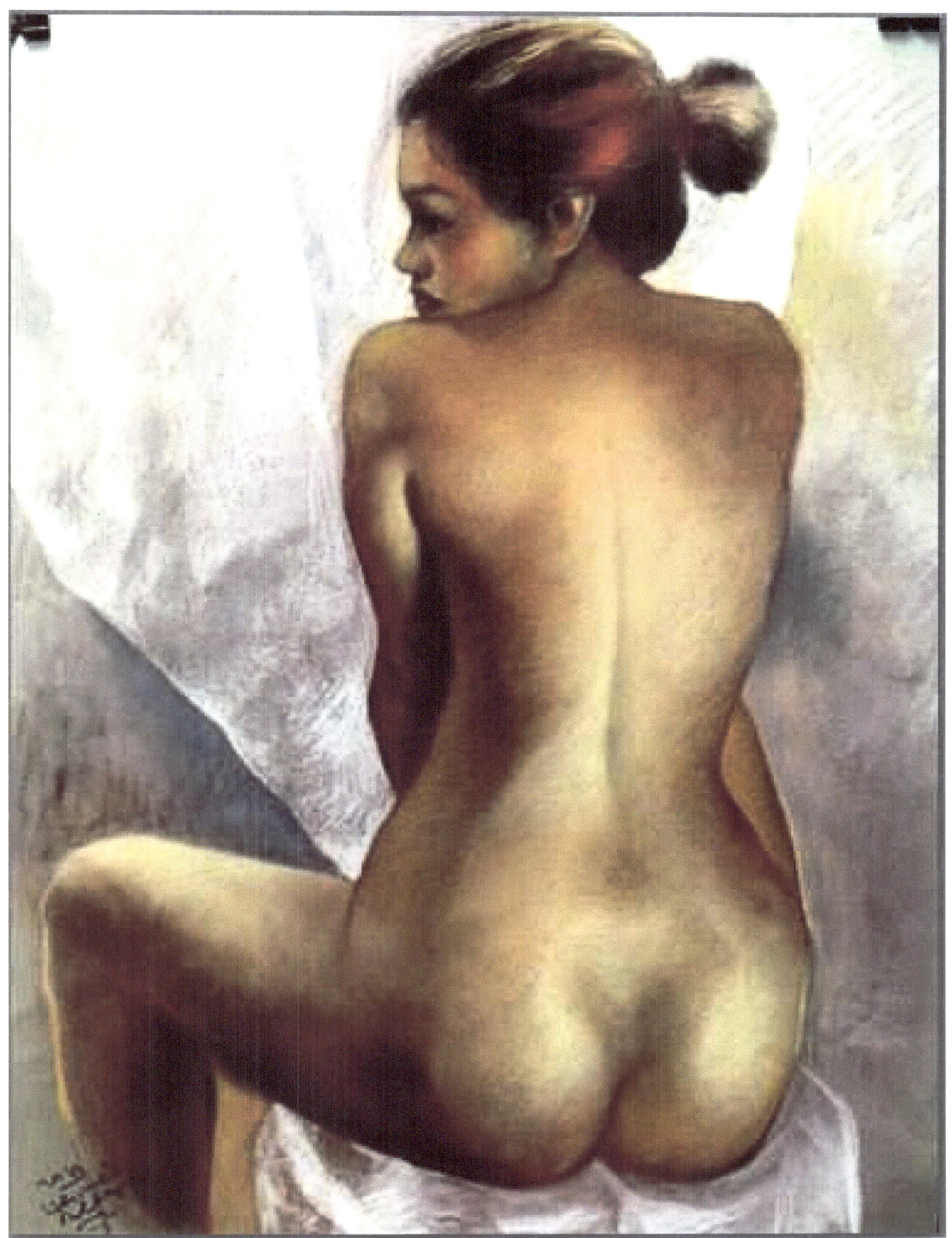

From Hermes Alegre Art Gallery Book-2

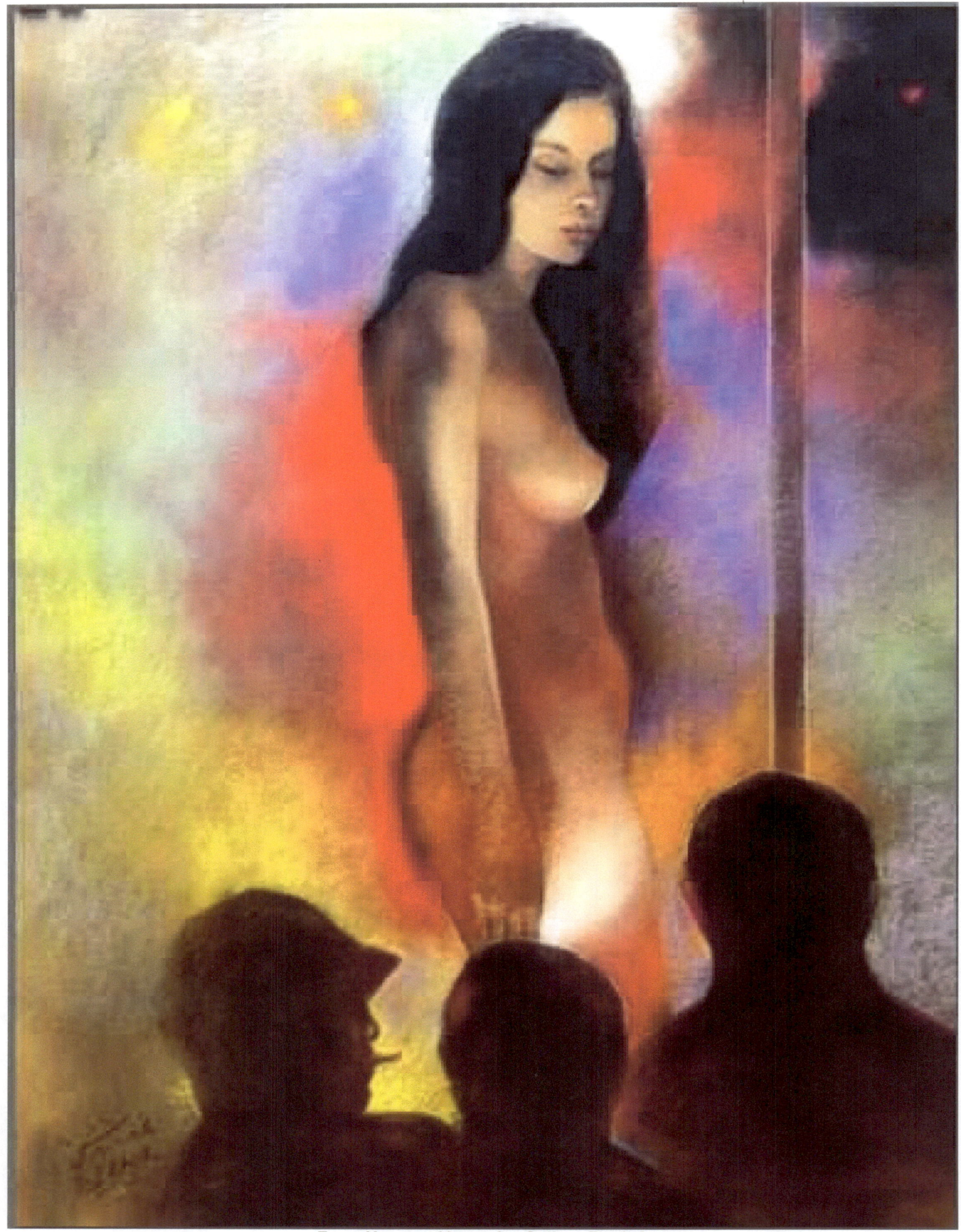

From Hermes Alegre Art Gallery Book-2

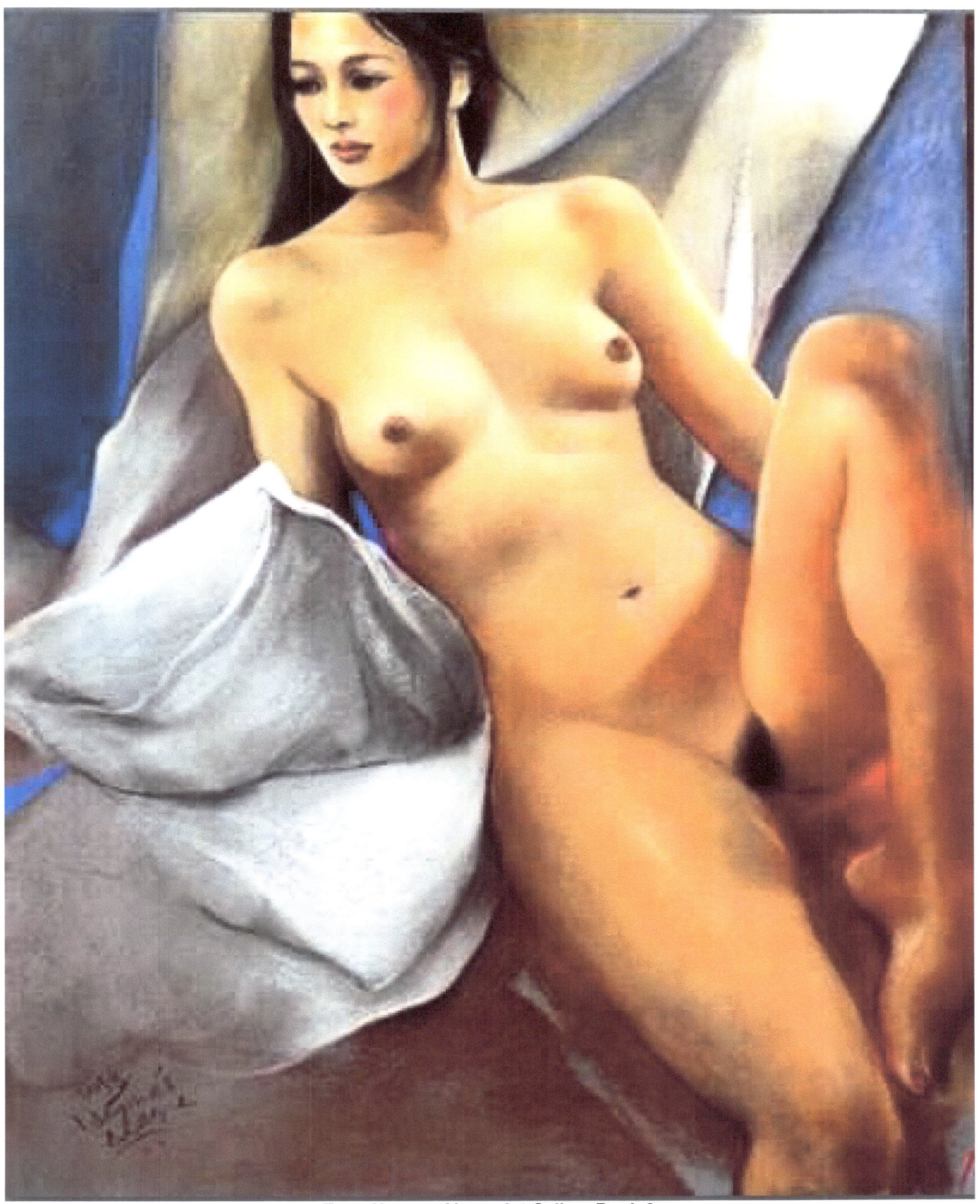

From Hermes Alegre Art Gallery Book-2

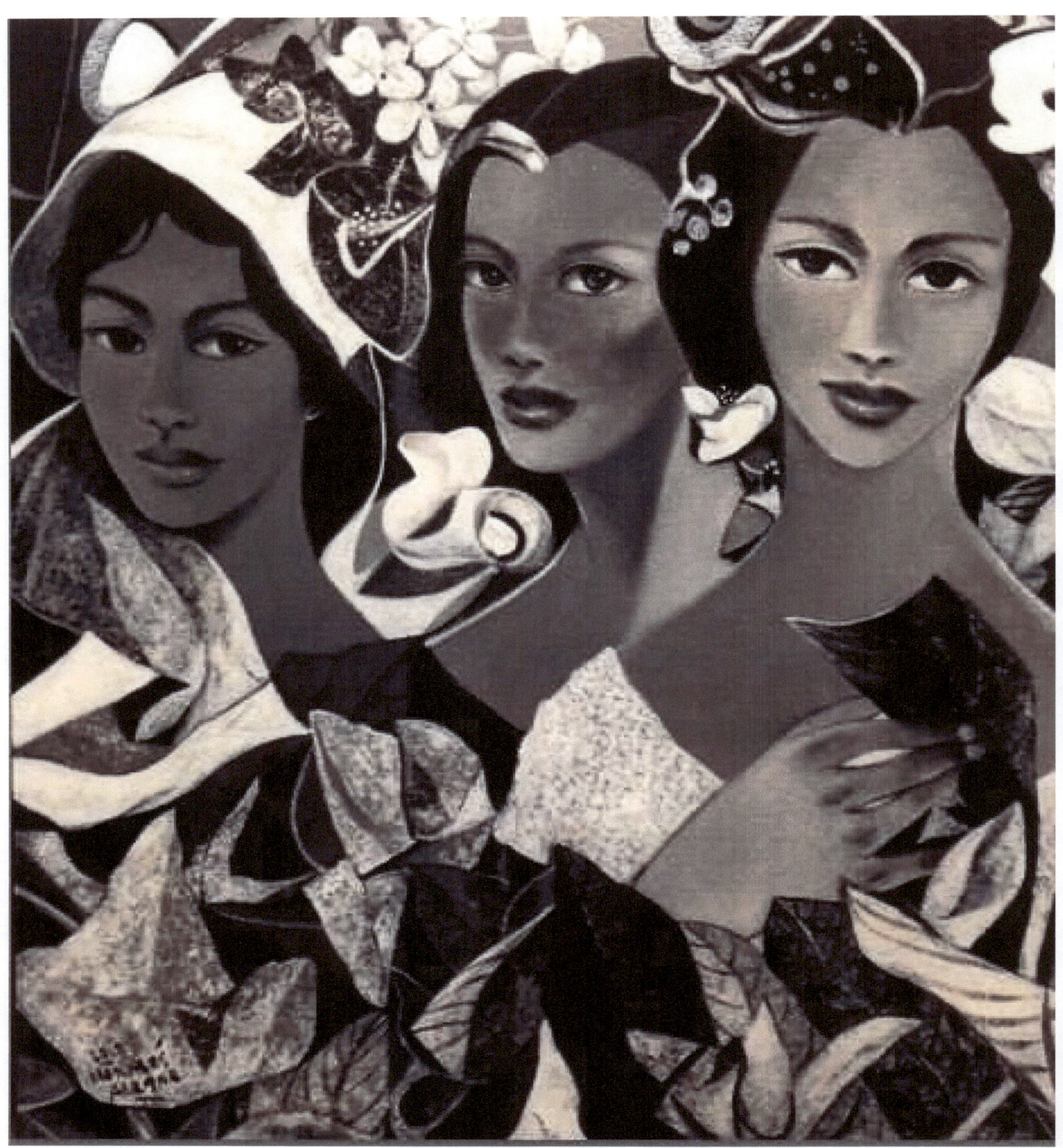

From Hermes Alegre Art Gallery Book-2

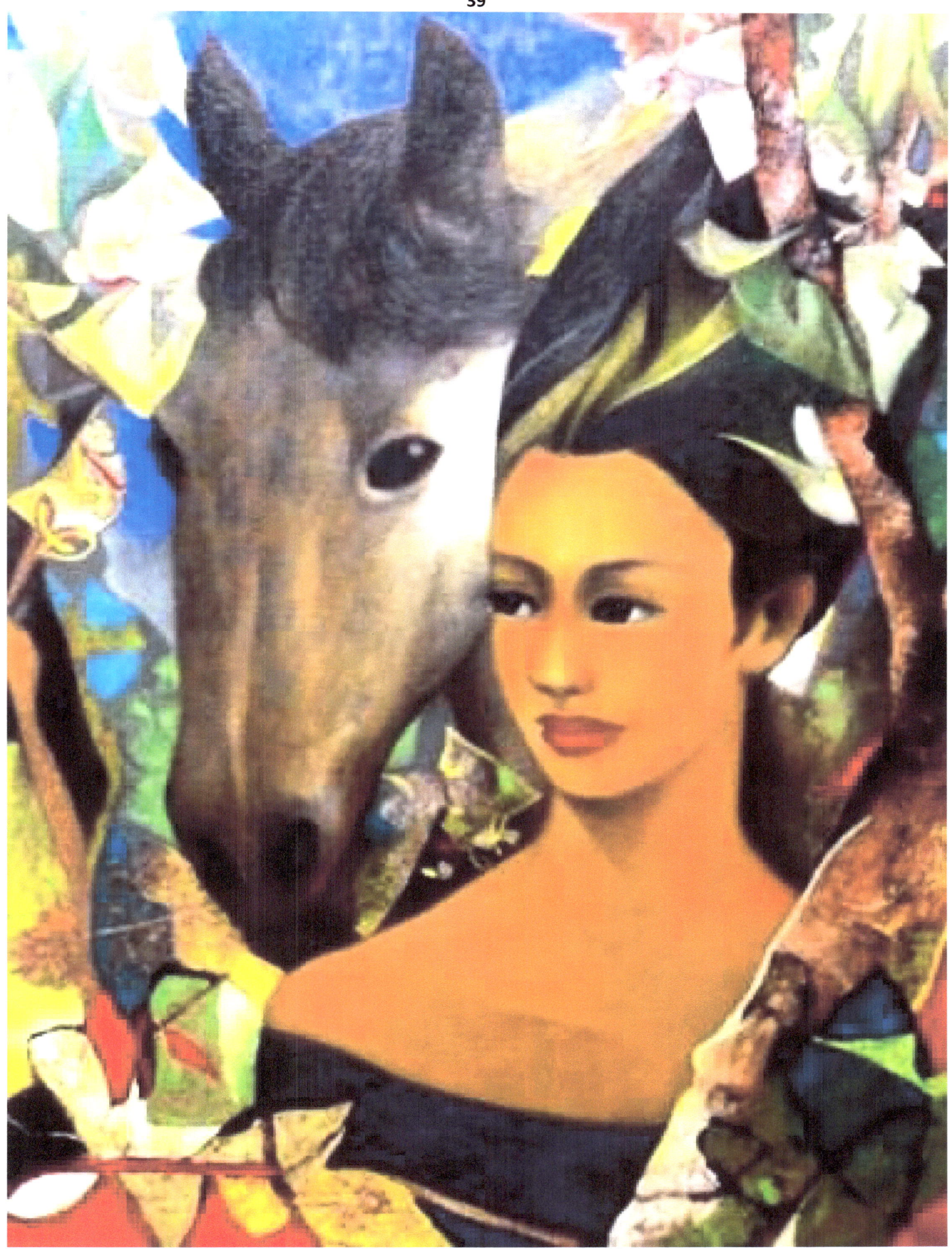

From Hermes Alegre Art Gallery Book-2

Published By Tatay Jobo Elizes
Publisher's List - Buy online as paperback or kindle, contact
job_elizes@yahoo.com, tatay@usa.com

Writings 1 Book, 2012 , Articles by Bambi Harper + Butch Jiimenez + Dr. Phil Stack + Noel Alegre + Toto Causing +_ Melanie Ferrer + Susie Barbieri _ Rodel Ramos + Sylvia Salvador + Tatay Jobo Elizes + + **Writings 2 Book, 2012,** Artices by Gov. Grace Padaca + Melanie Aquino + Toto Causing + Rodel Rodis + Cesar Torres + Joey Concepcion + Charity Guides + Cesar Lumba +_ Casiano Mayor Jr. + Sonny Coloma + Anonymous.+ + **Writings 3A Book, 2012**, Articles by Norman Madrid + Dr. Rene Azurin + Ernie Delfin + Toto Causing + Dr. Jose Abueva + MarVic Cagurangan + Casiano Mayor Jr + Rod Garcia + Roy Gaane + Tatay Jobo Elizes + + **Writings 3B Book, 2012,** Articles by Ceres Busa + John Reyes + Bert Guiang. + + **Writings 4A Book, 2012**, Articles by Dr Jose Abueva + Col. Dennis Acop + Fred Natividad + Irineo P. Goce, KaPule2 + Miguel Reynadlo + Marjorie Ann Elizes Reyes+ + **Writings 4B Book, 2012,** 1. Mi Ultimo Adios (My Last Farewell), *Dr. Jose P. Rizal* + 2. Aling Pagibig Sa Tinubuang Bayan, *Gat. Andres Bonifacio* + Articles by Irineo P. Goce or KaPule2 + + **Writings 5 Book -** **"Best Hopes" 2010 (About President P-Noy)**, Articles by Tony Meloto + F.SionilJose + Juan L. Mercado + OFWs Letter + Marcelo Tecson + Cesar Torres+ Perry Diaz + Dr. Philip S. Chua + Ernie Delfin + Atty. Ted Laguatan + Frank Wenceslao Jaileen F. Jimeno + Tatay Jobo Elizes + **Writings 6 Book, 2010** + I. SONA - State Of Nation Address - English - *Pres. Benigno Aquino III* + II. SONA - State of Nation Address - Pilipino - *Pres. Benigno Aquino III* + III. First 100 Days peech - Pilipino - *Pres. Benigno Aquino III* + **Artiucles by Bert Guiang** + Tony Meloto + Felicito or Tong C. Payumo + Cesar Lumba + Flor Lacanilao + Juan DelaCruz or Txtmanika + Dr. Ramon Marquez + Joey Jamito + Percival Cruz + Rod Garcia + Orion Perez Dumdum + Sarah Raymundo. + + **Writings 7 Book, 2010** - My Vintage Pics - Pictorials & Family, Tatay Jobo Elizes + + **Writings 8 Book, 2010,** Articles by Gel Santos Relos + Ms.Mike Portes + Jose Ma. Montelibano + Tony Meloto + Dr. Philip S. Chua + Dr. Cesar D. Candari + Dr. Eliseo Serina + Greg B. Macabenta + Irineo P. Goce or KaPule2 + Percival Cruz + Juan DelaCruz or Textmani + Demosthenes B. Donato. + + **Writings 9 Book, April 2011**, Articles by Judge Simeon dumdum Jr + Gemma Cruz Araneta + Larry Henares Jr + Tony Joaquin + Allen Gaborro + Atty. Toto Causing + Mar-Vic Cagurangn + Emily Espanol Derry, Poet + Elyn Jean Felarca, Poet + Naysan A. Albaytar + Laura Wade, Blogger + Perter Allan Mariano + Marge Trajeco-Aberasturi + Julia Carreon Lagoc + Irineo P. Goce or KaPulle2 + Anonymous. + + **Writings 10 Book, July, 2010**, Articles by Atty.Ted Lagutan + Percival C. Cruz + Allen Gaborro + Peter Allan Mariano + M.L. Munoz + Alvib T. Tabaniag + Resty Odon + Dr. Phili S. Chua + Dr. Cesar D. Candari + Anonymous. + + **Writings 11 Book, August, 2011** + 1, SONA In English and Filipino, by President Benigno Aquino III (P-Noy) + 2, Telltale Signs: SONA and the Dogfight Over Spratlys, by   Rodel Rodis + Atty. Ted Laguatan + Tatay Jobo Elizes + Jeremiah M. Opiniano + OFW Journalists + Bob & Carol Hammerslag + Roger P. Olivares + Rob Ceralvo + Anonymous + Irineo P. Goce or KaPule2 + Random. + + **Writings 12 Book, April 2012** + Articles By Orion Perez Dumdum + Julia C. Lagoc + Honorio M. Cruz, MD + Ben Gonzales, MD + Mar-Vic Cagurangan + Marisa Lerias + Gerry Partido + Dr. Cesar D. Candari + Erwin De Leon + Jovelyn B. Revilla + Tatay Jobo Elizes + + **Writings 13 Book, July 2012** + Articles by Raymundo E. Narag + M.L. Munoz + Sonia Barbara gl Munoz + Pamela Joy Agtoto + Percival C. Cruz + Tatay Jobo Elizes + Jhakie Eslit Bayobay + Reygel Saplad Perales.

Timely Writings 14, 2013 + Articles by Cesar F. Lumba + Eugenio Pulmano + Late Jesse Robredo + Antonio Nievera + Alvin T. Tabaniag + Kevin L. Nadal + Anonymous + Fred Natividad + Anonymous + Ellen Tordesillas + Lat Capt. Rene N. Jarque + + **Timeless Writings-15 (TW15), 2014** + Articles by SC Justice Antonio T. Carpio + Atty Dodel Rodis + Atty. Ted Laguatan + Sona by Pres. Benigno Aquino III + F. Sionil Jose + Dr. Philipi Stack + Racz Kelly, Padilla + Bert Armada.

Solo Authored Books: + + +

Book A, Turning Points, *Job Elizes Sr,1968 (Reissue 2009)* + + + Book B, Be Considerate For Once, *Tatay Jobo Elizes (Jr), 2013* Book C, Piglets Unlimited - Wealth, *Tatay Jobo Elizes, 2009* + + + Book D, Out of the Misty Sea We Must, *Cesar Lumba, 2010* + + + Book E, Fulfilled – *Gonzales Reynaldo, Editor, 2010* + + + Book F - Reflections - *Bert Guiang, 2010* + + Book G, Writings 7 - My Vintage Pics, *Tatay Jobo Elizes, 2010* + Book H, May Bagwis Ang Pag-ibig, *Percival C. Cruz* + + Book I, Letters To Matrimony, *Irineo P. Goce, Ka Pule2, 2011* + Book J, Songs I Wish You Knew, *Soledad R. Juan, 2011* + + + Book K, Make My Day, *Larry Henares Jr., 1993, Re-issue 2011* + Book L, Our Guerrero Family, *Tatay Jobo Elizes, 2010* + + + Book M, Handy Jokes, *Tatay J. Elizes, 2011* + Book N, FaveArt 1, *Tatay Jobo Elizes, 2011* + + Book O, Beyond idle thoughts, *MLMunoz, Sept,2011* + + + Book P, Cracks In The Armor, *Mariano Ngan, Oct 2011* + + + Book Q, FaveArt 2, *Tatay Jobo Elizes, 2011* + + Book R, Balitang Kutsero, *Perry Diaz, Jan 2012* + + Book S, FaveArt3, *Tatay Jobo, 2011* + + + Book T, FaveArt4 ,2012, *Tatay Jobo* + + + Book U, Stack Family Journals, *Phil & Fe Stack, 2012* + + + Book V, Emily, An Adoption Journey, *Romerl Elizes, 2012* + + + Book W, Hermes Alegre Art Gallery, *TJ & Hermes, 2012* + + + Book X, Masaya Din, Malungkot Din, *Jovelyn B. Revilla, 2012* Book Y, Tiis, Sipag At Tiyaga, *Raquel Delfin Padilla, 2012* + + + Book Z, Until I Meet You, *Jhackie Eslit Bayobay, 2012* + + + Book AA, Buhay At Pag-ibig, *Argel Lucero Tamayo, 2012* + + + Book AB, Hail to the Second Best, *Dr. Philip Stack, 2012* + + + Book AC, Life Bus, *Mommy Joyce Pineda-Faulmino, 2012* + + + Book AD, My Candid Musings, *Monette Dioquino Calugay, 2012* + Book AE, Tickets to Life, *Maria Lourdes Jesalva, 2012* + + + Book AF, The Dove Files, *Mike Portes, 2012* + + + Book AG, Nursing Vignettes, *Jocelyn Cerrudo Sese, 2012* + Book AH, Poor Ba Us, *R.A. Gubalane, 2012* + + Book AI, Summer Idyll, *Avelina Gil, 2012* + + Book AJ, Legacy (Pamana), *Rachel Astrero, 2012* + + Book AK, Narratives Old & New, *Avelina J. Gil, 2013* + + Book AL, Buhay Saudi, *Adele J. Esic, 2013* + + Book AM, Buhay Ofw Atbp, *Jessica Napat, 2013* + + Book AN, Mga Tula Ng Buhay, *Angelita C. Esguerra, 2013* + + Book AO, Not by Bread Alone, *Judge Lily V. Magtolis, 2013* + + Book AP, Jokes Collection-2, *Tatay Jobo Elizes, 2013* + + + Book AR, *My Writings Sometimes, Tatay Jobo Elizes, 2013* + + Book AS, Sa 'Yo Na Ako, *Shayne A. Martinez, 2013* + + Book AT, My Kin's Family Trees, *Tatay Jobo Elizes, 2013* + + Book AU, Rizal Family Tree & Others, *Tatay Jobo Elizes, 2013* + + Book AV, Make My Day-2, Nice & Nasty, *L. Henares, 2013 (1993)* + + Book AW, Make My Day-3, Cecilia, Love, *L.Henares, 2013 (1993)*Book AX, Handy Lyrics-1, *Tatay Jobo Elizes, 2013* + + Book AY, Ang Biblos, *Rev. Dr. Eugenio Guerrero, 2014 (1929)* + + Book AZ, Make My Day-4, *Sweet & Sour, L. Henares, 2014 (1993)* + + Book BA, Life's Journey, True Stories, *Dr. Phil Stack, 2014* + + Book BB, Gerry Gil Writings, 2014, *Danny Gil* + Book BC, Mr. President, *Hermie Rotea, 2014* + + Book BD, Nostalgic Pics 1, *Tatay Jobo Elizes, 2014* + + Book BE, MakeMyDay-5, Saints & Sinners, *Henares, 2014 (1993)* + Book BF, MakeMyDay-6, Villains & Heroes, *Henares, 2014 (1993)* + + Book BG, Nostalgic Pics 2 (ElizesClan), *TatayJE, 2014* + + Book BH, MakeMyDay-7, Tough & Tender, *Henares, 2014(1993)* + + Book BI, MakeMyDay-8, Light & Shadow, *Henares, 2014(1993)* + + Book BJ, MakeMyDay-9, Give & Take, *Henares, 2014(1993)* + + Book BK, MakeMyDay-10, ToBeOrNotToBe, *Henares, 2014(1993)* + Book BL,Emily Forever In Love, Poems,*Emily Espanol Derry, 2013* + + Book BM, The Sinatra Songbook, *Henares, 2014* + + Book BN, The Gaborro Reader, *Allen Gaborro, 2010* + + Book BO, *Ramon H. Lopez - Art Gallery, 2014* + + Book BP, Philippines Via Old Pics-1, *Tatay Jobo, 2014* + + Book BQ, *Ronna Manansala - Art Gallery, 2014* + + Book BR, **Philippines Via Old Pics-2,** *Tatay Jobo, 2014* + + Book BS, **Being Good-A Medley Of Love,** *Dr. Phil Stack, 2014* + + Book BT, **Lifestream Fisherman, A Filipino Odyssey,** *Paul Dalde, Jul2014* + + Book BU, *Kristina Reed Manansala, Art Gallery-1, August 2014.*

Publisher: Tatay Jobo Elizes was born in Manila, Philippines, in 1934, retiree, now based in NY, busy self-publishing and involved in piglets dispersal programs. Acknowledgement & Dedication: Gratitude and acknowledgment belongs to those who support my hobby publishing books and charities. I heartily dedicate this to my wife, Cora, my children, Tetchie, Chevy & Abeth, and Marie & Bimbo, my grandchildren, Karines & Aung, Noelle, Chad, Marjo, Jeb, Marvin & Marty, great-grandson Jason Win and Carson, my siblings Susan, Hilda, Bobby, Bey & Manny and to all my extended relatives and to all Filipinos.
Disclaimer: The Publisher disclaims any liability for the works of the Painter and Artist.

ISBN Code. Printed in the United States of America under ISBN code below.
ISBN-13: 978 - 1501038778   + + +   ISBN-10: 150103877X

Publisher's List - Contact job_elizes@yahoo.com, tatay@usa.com
My websites: http://tinyurl.com/mj76ccq + + + www.jobelizes.webs.com
"Buy A Book or Gift Somebody - paperback or kindle edition online"